LIFTOFF

INSPIRATION

The inspiration for *Liftoff: An Astronaut Commander's Countdown for Purpose-Powered Leadership* came when Colonel Rick Searfoss met Dr. Stephen R. Covey, author of *The 7 Habits of Highly Effective People*. Dr. Covey counseled, "You've got over twenty-five years of experience in what American businesses need more than anything else: leadership and teamwork. Share it." Since then, Rick has done just that, as a noted leadership speaker, consultant, and now, author.

Liftoff shares the insights of an astronaut commander leading the way. It will enable you to:

- *Employ a proven, balanced-leadership model in support of a greater purpose.*
- *Drive stellar operational results with a comprehensive, objective-centric execution system.*
- *Apply a countdown of twelve purposeful performance principles for outstanding outcomes.*
- *Strengthen your ability to lead and perform at the front lines to achieve mission success.*

LIFTOFF

Thought Leaders and Authors

"I've known Rick Searfoss for several years and am pleased that our orbits continue to cross regularly as we both support many exciting, innovative 'New Space' initiatives. Although in recent years human space missions might not have received as much public attention as during the Apollo Era, the requirements for the utmost in teamwork to survive and thrive in the supremely forbidding environment of space still remain.

Retired Colonel Rick Searfoss epitomizes the best of leadership for success in those enterprises, and in commanding STS-90 he carried on the finest traditions of the United States Astronaut Corps. He has magnificently captured the essence of that leadership in *Liftoff: An Astronaut's Countdown for Purpose-Powered Leadership*. It's a great read, shares important elements of the modern 'Right Stuff,' and will benefit those aspiring to lead."

—**Hon. Buzz Aldrin**, Colonel, USAF Retired, Astronaut and Distinguished Lunar Pioneer, Apollo XI and Gemini XII

"If you have a leadership mission to accomplish, you need to read *Liftoff* by space shuttle commander Rick Searfoss. His unique perspective on leadership in action will help you achieve 'execution excellence' no matter what task you are undertaking. Read this out-of-this world book and become a more successful leader here on earth!"

—**Ken Blanchard,** coauthor of *The New One Minute Manager*® and *Leading at a Higher Level*

"In *Liftoff*, Colonel Rick Searfoss powerfully shows how trust and purpose amplify effective leadership in the most dynamic of situations. While trust generates speed in changing everything for the better, trust *at* the kind of speed Rick has flown and in the team experiences he's had also provides us invaluable lessons for our own ventures. This real-world leader's take on what it takes to lead with integrity is simultaneously insightful and practical—and it really hits the mark. I highly recommend this tremendous book."

—**Stephen M. R. Covey**, *New York Times* and #1 *Wall Street Journal bestselling* author of *The Speed of Trust*

"Rick's own sterling leadership when we asked him to serve as Chief Judge for the original Ansari XPRIZE dovetails exactly with his purposeful and valuable take on the subject in *Liftoff: An Astronaut's Countdown for Purpose-Powered Leadership*. He reveals exactly what leaders must do to audaciously push the limits while keeping laser-like focus on achievable and essential targets.

Much like how we at the XPRIZE Foundation strive to be innovative catalysts for world-changing projects, Colonel Searfoss shows individual leaders how to do the same within their teams. A superb and valuable read for anyone hoping to lead for results that count!"

—**Peter H. Diamandis**, MD, Founder & Chairman of the XPRIZE Foundation, author of *New York Times* bestselling books *Abundance* & *BOLD*

"*Liftoff* brilliantly highlights the absolute need for courageous and aware leadership that focuses on daily execution even while keeping the insightful long-range view in mind. It digs down to the essence of getting the job done within teams for ultimate mission accomplishment to complete the positive transformations we envision in our organizations. Read it today to accelerate your team's success!"

—**Daniel Burrus,** author of *New York Times* bestseller *Flash Foresight*

"Rick Searfoss' new book gives new meaning to leadership. The content is profound, and the takeaways will change your execution formula forever! *Liftoff* not only does a deep dive into the 'who, what, when, where, why, and how,' but informs the reader how to leverage relationships to assure mission success. If this is the only book you read this year, don't miss it!"

—**Don Hutson**, #1 *New York Times* bestselling coauthor of *The One Minute Entrepreneur* and CEO, US Learning

"Few have led at a higher level—literally—or more challenging circumstances than space shuttle commander and test pilot Rick Searfoss. He shares action packed stories and lessons learned first-hand in some of the most exciting and interesting places imaginable. This book will push the envelope of your thinking. I recommend it."

—**Mark Sanborn**, bestselling author of *The Fred Factor* and *You Don't Need a Title to be a Leader*

"Most astronaut books start and end with 'Roger Houston, over and out' type of stuff. That is where Rick Searfoss is different. This shuttle commander has the biggest heart in NASA. Rick gets heart-led servant leadership. And he takes us to space and back to teach us these valuable lessons."

—**Tommy Spaulding**, *New York Times* bestselling author of *It's Not Just Who You Know* and *The Heart-Led Leader*

"In *Liftoff: An Astronaut Commander's Countdown for Purpose-Powered Leadership,* Colonel Rick Searfoss brings an amazing transfer of lessons learned from command in space to Earth-bound business settings. His concept of working the matrix of relationships aligns perfectly with my Platinum Rule* concept of always treating people the way they want and need to be treated. This leadership and team-building book is filled with a huge variety of pertinent lessons mixed with memorable, exciting stories from a successful former astronaut."

—**Dr. Tony Alessandra**, author of *The Platinum Rule* and *The NEW Art of Managing People*

"Astronaut Rick Searfoss knows how to skyrocket a team's productivity – literally! In *Liftoff,* he shares his hard-won secrets on how to execute exquisitely when the pressure is on. If you're serious about accelerating your team's performance to a SuperCompetent level, then climb aboard Rick's' rocketship and explore his valuable lessons on achieving real results."

—**Laura Stack**, MBA, CSP, President, The Productivity Pro, Inc., author of *Execution IS the Strategy*

"For over ten years I've been recommending Rick capture his amazing, heartfelt, high-content stories in a book. He's absolutely one of the best speakers on or off the planet, and now, finally, he has written a must-read masterpiece for anyone hoping to lead more effectively. *Liftoff* will change your life by giving you many new ways to influence others for good — there's one paragraph early in the book that I plan on reading every day for the rest of my life. Read and carefully apply his thorough, proven techniques!"

—**Frank Candy**, author and speaker,
Founder and President, American Speakers Bureau

"Wow! What an amazing set of true stories with profound and lasting impact. As an astronaut, Rick Searfoss has lived life at a performance level most of us can only dream about. Now, in his book *Liftoff: An Astronaut Commander's Countdown for Purpose-Powered Leadership*, he selflessly shares those incredible experiences to take us all to new levels of engagement and achievement. If you want to lead well, read this book!"

—**Curtis Zimmerman**, bestselling author of *Life at Performance Level*

Senior Business Leaders

"The concept of values-based leadership for a greater purpose is one that is needed now more than ever. *Liftoff: An Astronaut's Countdown for Purpose-Powered Leadership* is full of thought-provoking and useful principles for leading with purpose, and Colonel Searfoss brings them alive through engaging and unique stories.

With a background in common with Rick as a US Air Force Academy graduate and my experience starting and leading companies, I've seen firsthand over and over the power for good that leaders who exercise purposeful, values-based leadership can have. If you sincerely want to improve your leadership and also accomplish a mission beyond yourself, carefully consider and apply these lessons."

—**Bill Coleman**, Co-founder and former CEO, BEA Systems, Founder, former Chairman, and CEO, Cassatt Corporation

"Rick's incredible life journey has been on a path of outstanding, developed leadership qualities. I often work directly with him— he's a consummate team builder and people-oriented leader within our company and with our clients. Rick actively engages and leads for results with us and multiple other leading-edge flight test ventures. Dive into *Liftoff,* apply its lessons and learnings, and you too will truly lift off and succeed in your endeavors."

—Bill Korner, Founder and CEO, CompUSA, former CEO, Rand McNally, Chairman and CEO, Flight Research, Inc.

"Of the many leadership papers and books today, I lend my name only to *Liftoff* for one simple reason. It is only once in a rare while that you meet a single individual who combines proven leadership skills with world-class team building, drive, and results. As squadron mates and young eighteen-year olds, Rick and I survived the intense program of the United States Air Force Academy first year together. Even then, in a large pool of highly motivated and talented individuals, he stood out as a real leader of the highest integrity who really knew how to support and build others for the ultimate in teamwork.

His book captures the proven ideas of principle-centered behavior and 'dreaming big' but goes on to put theory into practice with actions like team preparation, drive, and persistence. I have seen Rick live these concepts, deliver results, and yet all the while keep his soul, his family, and his friends like no other person I have met. We will all be fortunate to learn his teachings."

—Mark Goebel, North America/Asia COO
and Managing Partner (retired), Accenture

"As a fellow Air Force Academy graduate and former fighter pilot, I thank Rick for his willingness to share the fundamental leadership principles from our common background mingled with the rare experiences from his command in space. What is most impressive is the splendid job he's done making those lessons so relevant to the business world! *Liftoff: An Astronaut Commander's Countdown for Purpose-Powered Leadership* is a must-read-and-heed work for those serious about leading in any venture."

—Paul Madera, Founder and Managing Partner, Meritech Capital, Number 7
on the Forbes Midas List of Venture Capital Investors

"A refreshing and valuable take on how leaders in the real world should act and serve. Colonel Searfoss, with his extensive operational background and distinctive command experiences in the space program, has done a marvelous job highlighting what all leaders in operational, on-the-line ventures must do for their teams to soar. *Liftoff* is truly a journey of inspiration!"

—**Peter F. Hartman**, Vice Chairman, Air France KLM

"Because we built our company from the ground up, I've learned firsthand what kind of leaders and teammates I can count on to make a difference. In *Liftoff,* Colonel Rick Searfoss superbly shares how to develop such effective leaders. More importantly, from his direct work with Luminox, we've seen how he 'walks his talk' and exemplifies what he teaches in his own leadership and team contributions!"

—**Barry Cohen**, Founder and CEO, Luminox Watches

"Rick Searfoss is a great American patriot, former astronaut, and shuttle commander. His leadership lessons remind me of that old adage: when the time to perform arrives, the time to prepare has passed. Colonel Searfoss understands and embraces ethics, teamwork, and preparation in order to be a leader. *Liftoff* is a great read for leaders at all levels. Rick has laid out a flight plan for all leaders who want to grow, succeed, and excel. I enjoyed reading it."

—**Howard Putnam**, former CEO, Southwest Airlines,
author of *The Winds of Turbulence*

"With the same exciting engagement and heartfelt expression we enjoyed when he shared his speaking message with our senior executives, in *Liftoff* Colonel Rick Searfoss explores in detail the central core of purposeful leadership. He provides great insights into the foundation for true leadership leading to the effective and efficient achievement of any mission or objective.

In our business, with a mission that truly does matter for patients worldwide, achieving our mission in the right way is of critical importance. The Colson Associates medical device member companies' employees around the world understand how purpose beyond ourselves really does bring out the best type of ethical and socially responsible leadership.

Rick's examples and guidelines are superb and relevant for all leaders, in any endeavor. I strongly encourage anyone interested in gaining valuable new insights into practical, effective leadership in business or in life to take the time to enjoy *Liftoff* and benefit from the unique perspectives Rick offers. The leadership strength that can be created from his focus on mission, accountability, and respect for individuals is powerful."

—**Louhon Tucker**, President and CEO, Colson Associates, Inc.

"Colonel Searfoss provides an engaging, unique perspective on the power of purpose in guiding effective execution toward a common goal."

—**William H. Rogers, Jr.**, Chairman and CEO, SunTrust Banks, Inc.

"For over a decade Rick Searfoss has been an uplifting inspiration to our Laserchrome Technologies team of designers, artists, and producers. He clearly possesses 'the leader's gifts' of integrity, faith, strength of character, realistic optimism, and good humor.

In *Liftoff: An Astronaut Commander's Countdown for Purpose-Powered Leadership*, Rick gives us his precise insight into a leader's process of decision making for outstanding performance. We enjoyed his remarkable ability to illustrate the complexities of leadership with lively, authentic analogies, vignettes, and narratives. By weaving together relevant illustrations from his own leadership journey, we encounter the dangers and challenges of his missions, his courage, and best practices for success. It's a powerful resource for all teams. If you want to lead better in business and in life, read and use *Liftoff*."

—**Emily Kubica**, President, Laserchrome Technologies, LLC

"Rick Searfoss provides a new and unique perspective on leadership. The discussions on teamwork, preparation, and purpose are important ingredients in the 'flight plan' for any business."

—**Mike Linton**, Chief Marketing Officer, Farmers Insurance, former CMO, eBay and Best Buy

World-Class Leaders, Performers, and Team Builders

"There's great reason why pilot astronauts are chosen from the ranks of fighter pilots: they have to lead and execute perfectly in the most dynamic, unforgiving environments imaginable. In *Liftoff: An Astronaut Commander's Countdown for Purpose-Powered Leadership*, Colonel Searfoss does a sterling job bringing home just how critical effective teamwork, leadership, and trust are not only in high performance cockpits, but down here on Earth in every business setting. 'Sierra Hotel' from liftoff to touchdown!"

—**Steve Ritchie**, Brigadier General, USAF Retired,
America's Last Fighter Pilot Ace, Congressional Gold Medal Recipient

"*Liftoff* is the first book that has taken the principles of aerospace, the teamwork of a mission, and the demands of NASA and made it into a compelling manuscript that will change how you lead your people. Colonel Rick Searfoss has captured time-tested principles that have been reinforced, mission after mission, and put them into language that even a former NFL running back could understand.

I had the privilege of working with Rick on a leadership seminar and walked away with the belief that whether you are on the playing field or in outer space, overcoming challenges requires essentially the same approach: applying the fundamentals with steadfast determination. Colonel Searfoss brilliantly shows teams how to be the best they can be and leaders how to persevere for meaningful achievement. Make sure you add *Liftoff* to your collection of playbooks."

—**Rocky Bleier**, Pittsburgh Steeler, 4 time Super Bowl Champion,
Vietnam Vet, author of *Fighting Back*

"Great leaders build great teams. Rick Searfoss has been creating, and then leading, great teams into space, where error would have fatal consequences. In my world, Everest and K2, we travel the same fine line between life and death. The practical laboratories of space exploration, mountaineering expeditions, or business have allowed folks like Rick and I to experiment with the key ingredients of team excellence in the face of great challenges. *Liftoff* details Rick's recipe for organizational excellence and will accelerate your team's journey to greatness."

—**Chris Warner**, CEO and Leadership Expert,
co-author of *High Altitude Leadership*

"Colonel Searfoss has done a great job of showing how he developed the full potential of his teams through the use of fascinating, real-world space exploration anecdotes. I am confident that *Liftoff* will assist you in achieving your own gold-medal leadership victories."

—**Jim Craig**, Goalie for the 1980 "Miracle on Ice" Olympic gold-medal US hockey team, bestselling author of *Gold Medal Strategies: Business Lessons from America's Miracle Team*

"In *Liftoff: An Astronaut Commander's Countdown for Purpose-Powered Leadership*, Colonel Rick Searfoss provides great insights into how a successful leader must balance risk and reward while inspiring a team to strive for the best. He shows us the true value of sticking our necks out in pursuit of accomplishments of worth and benefit to others. Inspiring and compelling—valuable on many levels."

—**Nikki Stone**, Olympic Gold Medalist, author of *When Turtles Fly: Secrets of Successful People Who Know How to Stick Their Necks Out*

Space Shuttle Colleagues

"*Liftoff* is a powerful 'checklist' for effective leadership of any size team or organization! Rick wraps his message around wonderful lifetime and space flight experiences that help cement his leadership lessons in the reader's mind.

I was blessed to be crewed with Rick on my last Space Shuttle flight and to witness him expertly exercise these fundamental leadership principles with great success—indeed, they culminated in him getting us home safely after a serious malfunction during launch. A must read!"

—**Kevin Chilton**, General, USAF Retired, former Commander, US Strategic Command and US Air Force Space Command, former NASA Astronaut and Space Shuttle Commander

"A wonderful leadership book from an astronaut commander has been a long time coming, and my crewmate Rick Searfoss is the perfect one to write it. As Rick's commander on his first mission, I had the privilege to witness not only his outstanding technical performance, but how he truly lived all the principles he writes about so well in *Liftoff.*

Rick's graciously shared expertise is born of deep real-world experience and the highest integrity in a lifetime of service. He was a joy to fly with in space.

You could count on him to faithfully perform all his responsibilities as second-in-command for space shuttle mission STS-58, and it's a joy to read his superb take on purposeful leadership, effective execution, and true teamwork."

—**John Blaha**, Colonel, USAF Retired,
former NASA Astronaut and Space Shuttle Commander,
former AVP, Applied Research, and AVP, Business Continuation, USAA

"Colonel Rick Searfoss is leading a life of success, excitement, and the stuff that dreams are made of! He knows what it takes to live a purpose-powered life and how to awaken those skills in those around him. Rick and I began working together over twenty-five years ago, before either of us were astronauts. We've flown together in the F-4, T-38, and gliders. We also completed initial astronaut training together in 'Group XIII' of the US Astronaut Corps.

Rick is a leader who consistently models the perfect blend of intense mission-oriented focus and inclusive, empathetic people skills. *Liftoff* magnificently shows how effective leaders must balance driving execution with caring for their team. Having shared the same leadership privilege as Rick of exercising command of human space missions, I can affirm how important that mix is to ultimate success. His techniques and stories are from a career that leaves little margin for error and, I believe, apply to all who desire a rewarding career and life experience. Applying his countdown principles will lift your leadership to higher levels!"

—**Eileen Collins**, Colonel, USAF Retired, former NASA Astronaut and first woman Space Shuttle Commander, Board of Directors Member, USAA

"Rick Searfoss was my first Shuttle Mission Commander. Rick was an outstanding leader who set the stage for me to build my career. From the first crew meeting until our final postflight debrief, he demonstrated the leadership principles he documents in *Liftoff*, ensuring our crew was ready to meet the inflight challenges we faced, and also ensuring that we could overcome each difficulty and make the flight the stunning success that it was. His example was a key part of the foundation I used to build on and lead my teams as I commanded the final two Hubble Space Telescope servicing missions.

Flying in space is truly a special privilege but also contains many challenges, from technical problems with the shuttle, problems with experiments that don't work as well in zero-gravity as on the ground, and the greatest challenge of all—keeping the team working well together, both in space and coordinating with the team on the ground. Rick's leadership set the standard for both developing our spaceflight team and interacting with Mission Control. Those same leadership lessons he demonstrated as my commander reverberate throughout *Liftoff* and make it a great read for any aspiring leader—or anyone who wants to see his own team's performance lift off!"

—Scott D. Altman, Captain, US Navy, Retired, Astronaut and Space Shuttle Commander, Group Vice President of Operations, ASRC Federal Engineering and Aerospace Solutions

LIFTOFF

An Astronaut Commander's Countdown for
PURPOSE-POWERED LEADERSHIP

COLONEL RICK SEARFOSS

Astronaut and Space Shuttle Commander

New York

LIFTOFF

An Astronaut Commander's Countdown for

PURPOSE-POWERED LEADERSHIP

© 2016 COLONEL RICK SEARFOSS.

Published in New York, New York, by Morgan James Publishing. Morgan James and The Entrepreneurial Publisher are trademarks of Morgan James, LLC.
www.MorganJamesPublishing.com

The Morgan James Speakers Group can bring authors to your live event. For more information or to book an event visit The Morgan James Speakers Group at www.TheMorganJamesSpeakersGroup.com.

A **free** eBook edition is available with the purchase of this print book.

CLEARLY PRINT YOUR NAME ABOVE IN UPPER CASE

Instructions to claim your free eBook edition:
1. Download the BitLit app for Android or iOS
2. Write your name in **UPPER CASE** on the line
3. Use the BitLit app to submit a photo
4. Download your eBook to any device

ISBN 978-1-63047-662-5 paperback
ISBN 978-1-63047-663-2 eBook
Library of Congress Control Number:
2015907788

Cover Design by:
Rachel Lopez
www.r2cdesign.com

Interior Design by:
Bonnie Bushman
bonnie@caboodlegraphics.com

In an effort to support local communities and raise awareness and funds, Morgan James Publishing donates a percentage of all book sales for the life of each book to Habitat for Humanity Peninsula and Greater Williamsburg.

Get involved today, visit
www.MorganJamesBuilds.com

Habitat
for Humanity®
Peninsula and
Greater Williamsburg
Building Partner

To Julie, with love eternally.
Your support, patience, and sacrifices
far beyond my own let me live the dream.

TABLE OF CONTENTS

ILLUSTRATIONS

FOREWORD

Duane H. Cassidy, General, US Air Force Retired, former Commander, Military Airlift Command and US Transportation Command, former Senior Vice President, Sales and Marketing, and Chief Commercial Officer, CSX Transportation

For the past sixty-one years, since being commissioned as an officer in the United States Air Force, I have been fascinated by the term and subsequent execution of *leadership*. In many speeches I have attempted to lead those in the audience to differentiate between Leadership and Management. As our world has become much more technical, management seems to have trumped leadership as an evaluation tool to measure success or failure in getting the job done, whatever its nature. To that point, I paraphrase a quote from Lord Slim of the British Army as he declared that management is a science of numbers and calculations, and the evaluation of same, useful to history and planning. Whereas leadership, according to Slim, is of the mind and of the heart and of the spirit: it is about relationships between the leader and those led. He suggests that "…management is necessary—leadership is essential."

If you appreciate this distinction regarding leadership, you are going to love *Liftoff: An Astronaut Commander's Countdown for Purpose-Powered Leadership*, by Rick Searfoss. Much has been written on leadership in this era following more than twelve years of ground combat in Iraq and Afghanistan, as well as a decade long air campaign prior. I know of no other volume as this, written by an astronaut who literally takes you out of this world to demonstrate the value, importance, and essential nature of good leadership. He gives you formulas to consider in your responsibilities as the leader and tools to guide you and help you assess your own leadership. The book is crammed with processes and tools such as the 4P Leadership Performance Balance. It will take you through a twelve point countdown of key performance principles for understanding and application. It also provides a path to look back and see if your successes are a product of happenstance: are people following out of curiosity or are you the engaged leader worthy of greater responsibility and continuation?

One should understand just what sort of guy Rick Searfoss, the fighter pilot, test pilot, and astronaut, really is to fully appreciate his thoughts and beliefs on leadership. I offer this perspective since there is no one on earth who has known Rick longer than I. His dad, Air Force retired Lieutenant Colonel Jerry Searfoss, and I were deployed together as brand-new second lieutenant navigators on a type of Air/Sea Rescue airplane, the SA-16, to Eniwetok Atoll during Operation Redwing, the 1956 hydrogen weapons tests. We were gone for over seven months and just prior to our return, Rick was born. Coming home, I landed one day before Jerry, and therefore met baby Richard even before his father did. From that day until now, despite long periods where both were engrossed in Air Force duties far apart geographically, and on mission, we have enjoyed a deep friendship as the Four Star and the Astronaut.

I had the pleasure of watching Ricky (that's what our kids called him) grow up, though there were times it was not at all certain he would. Our families were stationed together through several assignments. His father and I both became pilots and flew airlift/transport airplanes, resulting in many long, absent-from-home missions, particularly during times of crisis around the world during the Cold War. Rick, terribly smart and determined, always had his own ideas on how, when, and where things should be done, many of which did not coincide with his mother's. She was running things at home while we were off flying airplanes from the C-121 to the B-47 and KC-135. Young Rick challenged her regularly, learning recurring lessons about acceptable behavior and the meaning of "your dad will hear about this when he returns." Rick has always been intense, focused, and driven, whether challenging his mother's leadership at home or commanding a space shuttle mission. His intense focus is tempered by unflagging positivity and good humor.

Rick was and is driven to succeed. Early on, it was clear he would succeed at whatever interested him, and *everything* interested him. Number one in his class at the Air Force Academy, he also got his pick out of pilot school based on class ranking, and later was selected as instructor pilot of the year flying the F-111. He represented the Air Force magnificently when we sent him on exchange to the Navy's Test Pilot School. Rick never considered the sky to be the limit, making the natural next step to NASA and becoming an astronaut. It had been obvious to those of us in his world for more than twenty-five years that Rick really did have "the Right Stuff."

Now Rick has shared his thoughts on leaders and leadership, and detailed his belief that those privileged to be called to leadership should rise to the occasion. Rick lays his theories before us as a good engineer would, but he makes the telling so interesting and exciting, you won't realize what he's doing. They are borne out by the exciting anecdotes that only an astronaut who has experienced so much could share. His teachings are adaptable and essential, whether used in the world of commerce, a nonprofit organization, leading a battalion of the 82nd Airborne, a thirty-second spacing flow of airlift airplanes, or as the senior leader of the entire Air/Land operation, the CEO. They would also fit nicely in the planning and execution of the operation to land the first astronaut with the American flag on Mars. Rick's experiences, along with his ability to codify them into useful thoughts and behavior, are worthy of your time and consideration.

When you finish reading *Liftoff*, you too will know Rick Searfoss and understand why he has my utmost respect and pride.

Preface

THE COMPELLING
NEED FOR YOU TO LEAD

Do you feel a compelling need to lead? No matter who you are, you should! The world cries out for you to lead, and lead with purpose. Specifically, your company, team, community, volunteer organization, friends, family, and any team of which you are part all truly need you to exercise meaningful influence. At its core, leadership is simply influencing others for good. More than ever in this chaotic and confusing world, those who courageously offer sincere, service-oriented, and effective leadership succeed in guiding others to produce results that matter. Whether you are a senior executive, a supervisor at the operational level, the newest hire, or even "just" a neighborhood volunteer, you unquestionably can and should exercise leadership initiative.

This book doesn't attempt to define what exact difference you should make; that's clearly up to you. It does, however, offer practical, tested means for you to bolster your ability to accomplish your mission with others. We all need to engage in making the right things happen through skillful, effectively led execution. It's woefully inadequate to suppose oneself a "thought leader," issue lofty generic guidance, and expect tangible results. Conversely, it's an abrogation of your potential just to sit back through fear or lack of drive and let others do all the heavy leadership lifting. Regardless of your position, you can make a real difference if you proactively apply the correct principles to positively influence others at the execution-action level.

I trace this book's genesis to meeting Dr. Stephen R. Covey, author of *The 7 Habits of Highly Effective People: Powerful Lessons in Personal Change*, when I was a senior astronaut preparing to move into the business world. He counseled me that with all my leadership and teamwork experiences, I'd find multiple ways to contribute. After that transition, I saw his wisdom firsthand and grew more compelled to share my unique experiences to promote and build leaders and teams. For over a decade now, I've engaged as an expert professional business speaker with the mission of "sharing the leadership, teamwork, and innovation lessons of human spaceflight to launch organizations to higher heights of execution performance." This book extends and expands that mission, taking an even deeper dive into the world of execution leadership than I can possibly make during an hour on the speaking platform.

With my background as a leader in dynamic, challenging, and often dangerous operational environments, I envisioned this book as a "do leader's" guide to executing well. While the experiences from flying in space are unique, the principles for success in that venture are universal and applicable in any undertaking. The book's purpose is to present effective execution-leadership principles with examples from both the wondrous endeavor of human spaceflight and more typical earthbound settings. My models, systems, and stories all have the purpose of helping you and your teams execute more effectively.

While I've attempted to provide as comprehensive a treatment of purpose-powered leadership in this book as possible, I'd love to share more resources to help you on your own leadership development journey. The websites www.ricksearfoss.com, www.liftofftoleadership.com, and www.astronautspeaker.com all supplement the book's content. These resources include related imagery, video, blogs, the Countdown of Purposeful Performance Principles, and more.

So here is your call to action: commit to lead for real results, with purpose and passion! I sincerely hope this book boosts your ability and desire to do so.

ACKNOWLEDGMENTS

Writing this book has been simultaneously exhilarating and exhausting. It was exhilarating to fondly recall the many phenomenal experiences I've enjoyed and especially the great people with whom I shared them. The process also proved exhausting in striving to capture both excitement in the storytelling and worthwhile content for the reader. Along that trajectory, many family members, close friends, and colleagues boosted the project and kicked it into orbit.

Like me, my family did not at first fully appreciate the commitment required to complete a book until I finally buckled down and went for it. Unlike me, however, they were filled with unbridled confidence from the start that we could accomplish this mission. That reinforcement never wavered from any of them. I dedicate this book to my loving wife Julie, whose care, kindness, and perseverance know no bounds. Thank you, Julie, for every single moment together. To our oldest daughter Megan and her husband Devin, both wise beyond their years, thanks for continual, insightful, and pertinent critiques. Liz, I appreciate your perky, encouraging query every single time you called and asked, "Dad, how's the book going?" Camille, our nothing-is-impossible youngest, thanks for supporting me with an attitude that expressed, "Of course Dad can write a great book, why not?" Though they certainly don't realize it, my three young grandsons,

Liam, Duncan, and Malcolm, provided needful breaks from the writing plus inspiration that the book should leave a legacy for them too.

My own parents, Jerry and Mary Kay Searfoss, as well as my stepmother Barbara, offered wisdom without which I'd never have had the chance to become an astronaut or find the content for this book. Mom, I continually count the blessings of your teachings and wistfully reflect that if you hadn't passed so young, you could've seen the fruit they bore. Dad, thanks for still being there as a stalwart example of the best a man should be. Your example of service-beyond-self as a US Air Force officer set me on my path.

Foremost among business mentors who helped me with the content of the book are my sister and brother-in-law, Debbie and Jesse Armstrong. Those years of gaining hard-won wisdom in the real business world while I was off "slipping the surlies" in the Air Force and NASA enabled them both to help me focus my message. Similarly, Frank Candy, Chris Ayers, Dennis Falci, Tommy Spaulding, Mark Sanborn, and Wally Adamchick, I appreciate all your very astute comments. Thanks also to my niece and professional graphic artist Katie Sparkman for her work bringing my cover and diagram visions to reality.

I owe a special debt of gratitude to those with whom I shared the dream of flying in space: STS-58 crewmates, John Blaha, Bill McArthur, Rhea Seddon, Shannon Lucid, Dave Wolf, and Marty Fettman; STS-76 team, Kevin Chilton, Rich Clifford, Shannon Lucid (twice, what fun!), Ron Sega, and Linda Godwin; *Mir* cosmonauts, Yuri Onufrienko and Yuri Usachev; and my own STS-90 crew, Scott Altman, Kay Hire, Rick Linnehan, Dave Williams, Jay Buckey, and Jim Pawelczyk. Beyond your phenomenal technical talents, your wisdom, humanity, leadership, and friendship have touched me even more profoundly than the spaceflight experience itself. I'm also grateful for everyone with whom I worked in the Space Shuttle Program and during my service in the US Air Force. Collectively, you all helped lay the foundation for most of this book.

I love working with world-class performers in any field. As a first-time author, I'm deeply grateful for the experienced professionals at Morgan James Publishing and our editing partners, Split-Seed Editing. David Hancock and Amanda Rooker, I appreciate your affirmations that the book has value for the public, something important to say, and that I expressed myself reasonably well—even before we unleashed your folks to make it better. Managing editors, Margo Toulouse and Angie Kiesling, thanks for keeping this rookie on task and on time. To my copy editors, Cheryl Ross and Jennifer Hanchey, thank you for helping me keep the unique astronaut voice as a writer while clarifying and cleaning up the manuscript magnificently. Jim Howard, Morgan James Director of Operations, thanks for your incredible branding advice and perceptively pinning down the perfect title after I'd gone through nearly a hundred iterations. Finally, for everyone else on the Morgan James team, thanks for being such a superb "dream crew."

Introduction

USING THIS BOOK, YOUR FLIGHT DATA FILE

"Alone we can do so little; together we can do so much."
—Helen Keller

Leadership and team execution fundamentals are universal and apply to any venture. This book distills these foundational aspects into twelve key principles within four categories: Purpose, People, Perspective, and Program. Emphasizing purpose and program, it presents a practical system to boost effective execution at the point of action for purpose-powered results.

Your Flight Data File
The Flight Data File (FDF) for a space shuttle mission is the sum total of all the onboard documentation. It consists of checklists, manuals, cue cards mounted around the cockpit, flipbooks securely attached to special mounting brackets for launch and reentry, and programs and data loaded into as many as a dozen laptop computers for use in orbit. Every flight phase has a different FDF configuration

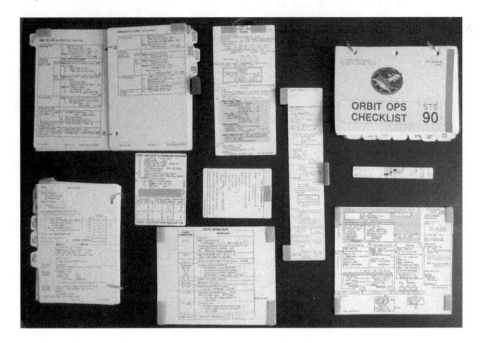

so the crew can readily reference all the procedures and information required to do the job.

Throughout training, astronaut crews spend an incredible amount of time reviewing the FDF. Now it's time to introduce you to the FDF for your upcoming launch to explore execution leadership and teamwork: this book. It'll be helpful to know the overall "flight plan." I'll explain what the book is, or at least what it intends to be, and what it definitely is not. Finally, we'll review how to use particular features, some included as a fun nod to my space background, and all intended to concisely reinforce key points.

This Book's Mission

This book is not an astronaut memoir. I do fully recognize the rarity of those experiences I've enjoyed and believe all the execution leadership principles I've learned and practiced are relevant in any business operation. Furthermore, the privilege of serving in many organizations with meaningful missions has informed my outlook on the power of purpose to guide effective execution. This book includes personal stories and space metaphors to support its mission of presenting leadership and teamwork principles you can use to execute *your* mission effectively. If you would like some additional perspective on how this particular astronaut/commander/author came by his approach to execution leadership and teamwork, I've shared personal background at the end of this text.

The 4P Leadership Performance Balance

Many years ago, in searching for a universal organizing framework for understanding effective leadership and teamwork, I developed a model I call the 4P Leadership Performance Balance. The 4P model recognizes that, almost without exception, the necessary elements for success in any undertaking fall into these four divisions: Purpose, People, Perspective, and Program. The framework applies to individual performance, leadership, team structure, and execution activities. Leaders must address all the elements without neglecting any. It has served me very well across a broad variety of endeavors with different companies and nonprofit organizations to which I contribute.

In over a thousand presentations worldwide, I've nearly always employed the 4P model for organizing structure. Audiences connect well to dividing content that way. However, the categories certainly do not exist in pristine independence. Every single one relates to all the rest. Elements overlap and interconnect. Graphically, you can represent the 4P model like those seventh grade math Venn diagrams of overlapping bubbles. Figure 1 depicts the model.

4P LEADERSHIP PERFORMANCE BALANCE

Figure 1

The 4P approach creates the flight plan for a trajectory or arc to present principles and examples of leadership for purpose-driven execution. Accordingly, the book has four major parts (I-IV), each representing one of the four Ps. Across these sections, the chapters count down from twelve to one. Action verbs figure prominently in each chapter title to reflect the specific, purposeful orientation you should have and the type of execution excellence activities you should undertake. Don't let the reverse chapter numbering confuse you. How else should one do a countdown?

Because of extensive overlaps and parallels across categories, teams may not necessarily exercise the principles from them in strict sequence. In the messy world of the human workplace, teams don't operate in pure linearity, neatly marching through one category of activities at a time. The real world unforgivingly does not allow such sequential execution orderliness. At any given time in its existence, a team could easily be cranking out work with various projects or initiatives tied to any of the four categories.

Program: The PAPA Effective Execution System

Each of the first three Ps—Purpose, People, and Perspective—has two chapters. The first part of the book generally covers stage-setting concepts, team formation, and people-building activities to set the team up to execute well. In addition to leading off the book, purpose also infuses every single chapter because continually reflecting on the "why" informs effective execution. In keeping with the active execution focus Program, or how you actually get the mission done, takes up the last six chapters.

Program also has its own detailed model I developed: the PAPA Effective Execution System. PAPA stands for Preparation, Awareness, Persistence, and Accountability. Graphically, you can represent this model like our planetary system. The pertinent, mission-supporting objectives form the home planet Earth at the center; the four individual PAPA satellites surround and must align with the objectives, much like the Earth's gravity holds the moon and manmade satellites in alignment. As leaders transit from satellite to satellite in execution, they must do so at just the right pace, continually returning to each and employing correct principles along the way. The Part IV introduction will more fully introduce this system. Chapters 6 through 1 address, in detail, how to apply each aspect of this repeating cycle during operational execution.

The two key models connect conceptually as well. You can envision purpose as the light and warmth of the sun, bathing the entire system and thus providing context and meaning to everything else. Think of people as those down on Earth we serve and also our teammates on our orbital journey. Finally, perspective gets us up off the home planet to look back and see the big picture. Figure 2 diagrams the PAPA system, how it connects with the 4P model, and how the chapters correspond to each aspect.

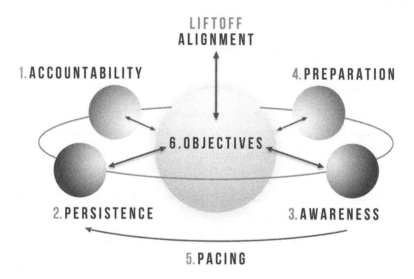

THE PAPA EFFECTIVE EXECUTION SYSTEM

Figure 2

The Countdown of Purposeful Performance
Principles to Guide Execution

Presented at the very beginning of each chapter is an overarching and explicitly stated Purposeful Performance Principle. Coupled with the action-oriented titles, these principles define the core of what I hope the reader will take away and apply. They are my personal summary of classic and timeless guidelines, filtered through a full career of my own team and leadership applications. They certainly did not just pop into my head while floating around in zero gravity!

I believe constant reminders of the basics are what we all need in our endeavors. The principles are basic blocking and tackling, and it's best just to lay them out there. Universal relevance then comes from applying fundamentals in a wide variety of ventures. Any unique take in this work will come from the expansion and reinforcement of the concepts via distinctive and memorable experiences in dynamic, real-world settings.

To introduce these principles and compile them in one place, here is the countdown:

Purposeful Performance Principles:

Purpose
12. Actively seeking and embracing difficult challenges gives powerful initial direction, informs the vision, and encourages the team.
11. A meaningful cause in service to others inspires team members to fully commit to mission accomplishment.

People
10. Constant care of the matrix of both internal and external relationships amplifies team unity and leverages effective collaboration.
9. More than any single factor, a high-trust culture enables capturing people's best efforts and contributions to meet the most challenging commitments.

Perspective
8. A positive yet reality-grounded perspective sets the stage for highest team member engagement, productivity, and results.
7. Adherence to values-based principles prevents drift and systematically keeps execution on track during preparation, action, and follow-through.

Program
6. Achieving correctly defined, well-developed, and suitably emphasized objectives empowers the team to fulfill the mission, turning vision into reality.

5. Pushing ahead diligently, with a long-range view, opportunities orientation, and optimal pace, fosters the responsiveness to stay ahead of problems and competitors.

4. Deep preparation and guarding against complacency in planning, training, and briefing accelerate the team into effective action.

3. Peak productivity takes superb knowledge and competence, strong situational awareness, and a relentless drive to improve.

2. Leading all the way to successful completion requires tenacious persistence, acting in alignment with objectives, wisely mitigating risks, and patiently adjusting operations.

1. Execution excellence demands total accountability, principled adaptability, and a disciplined debriefing mindset.

Practical, Not Theoretical

The best teamwork and leadership practices are comprehensive and practical, particularly when it comes to actual execution process and technique. Regardless of the specific venture, certain fundamental axioms apply. In working with clients and presenting to audiences the last ten years, I've discovered in great detail the many operational challenges they face. That discovery process has proven heartening due to the similarities at the core of every endeavor, regardless of industry or company. One might consider it a must in writing yet another book on a popular business topic to create an entirely new take on it. Given that this work is the first business leadership book from an astronaut, it certainly does have unique elements. I also believe that the hybrid combination of a purposeful orientation with the action of execution presents the topic in a new light. What I believe is most valuable, though, is expressing through a wide variety of applications the most important principles.

Just two months after commanding Space Shuttle Mission STS-90 on *Columbia*, I spoke to an audience of twenty-two thousand people at America's Freedom Festival in Provo, Utah. Although I did not realize it at first, Dr. Stephen R. Covey, author of *The 7 Habits of Highly Effective People* and by then a worldwide-recognized thought leader, was in the audience. My host introduced me to him at a reception following the public event. It was an honor. I had carefully read his practical and empowering work when it first came out, and I have consciously attempted to live its principles. I indicated to Dr. Covey how valuable I'd found using those habits in preparing the crew and our support teams to complete the mission successfully. He was extremely gracious, even inquiring if he could quote one of the points I had made in an upcoming book. Of course, I said yes!

As we continued our discussion, I explained that I was considering retiring from the Astronaut Corps and was interested in pursuing a second career in the business world. Expressing some concern to Dr. Covey, I said, "I'm a pretty technical guy, with my degrees in aero engineering and aeronautics [a specialized applied physics degree], so I'm worried about adapting to the business environment." He looked at me a little quizzically, then replied, "You've got over twenty-five years of experience in what American businesses need more than anything else: leadership and teamwork. Share it!"

I've consistently found that the fundamental leadership and teamwork principles I've been privileged to practice in a career of executing in dynamic, stressful flying environments apply perfectly well in a business setting. Furthermore, I believe a full career in service to our great nation as a military officer and astronaut has sensitized me to service beyond self in pursuit of a meaningful purpose. Dr. Covey's words to me back in 1998 expressed confidence that as an astronaut and mission commander, I have appreciable understanding, insights, and expertise to offer business teams. Feedback and continuing engagement with clients reinforces the universality of that expertise.

Throughout the years, I've also continued my own diligent study of the art and practice of leadership and business execution, reading extensively on the subject to expand my ability to help clients. Generally, these works fall into one of two categories: the academic study or the more hands-on approach from someone who's "been there, done that." Graduate business school professors and other academic types often have profound acumen regarding leadership and organizational development. Many leaders from the business world, or from backgrounds like sports, mountain climbing, and the like, have also offered deep insights and useful perspectives. I thoroughly enjoy reading both types of books.

A good friend and Air Force Academy classmate, Gordy Curphy, clearly fits as a noted academic leadership expert. Gordy has a PhD in industrial/organizational psychology and coauthored one of the most widely used leadership volumes in MBA programs nationwide, *Leadership: Enhancing the Lessons of Experience*. He also understands the practical side of leadership. Gordy played varsity hockey, served with distinction as an Air Force personnel officer after graduation, was later a professor at the Academy, and subsequently became president of a nationwide HR consulting firm.

A few years back, Gordy and I were hanging out and catching up. By then, both of us had transitioned to serving clients in our own businesses, me with corporate speaking and Gordy with consulting and executive coaching at CEO and boardroom levels. As we laughed and reminisced about our cadet days and experiences, we noted how important that foundation had been for our current professional activities. Having read Gordy's intense, five hundred-plus page academic tome, I marveled about his depth of knowledge in the field and how valuable his teachings were. His response: "Rick, that's all well and good, but you've got the stories and experiences to take a different but equally useful path, writing as a 'troubadour' leadership expert. You should do a book; put those stories and lessons from your speeches down on paper." He elaborated, explaining that the troubadour couples axioms with fun stories to hold the reader's attention and may strike a more responsive chord with business people than would a pure content data dump. "Get on with it, Rick!"

I clearly fit into the troubadour mold when it comes to sharing practical leadership and execution lessons. I don't have a painstakingly earned PhD after my name like Gordy and his professor colleagues, who've devoted full careers to drilling deeply into the root causes and effects of organization and individual development. I have studied the literature in the field extensively and enjoyed the advantage of comparing notes with many hundreds of business clients and team leaders through the years. Although that study has given me a keen appreciation for the incredible academic body of knowledge in organizational development, I'm neither equipped for nor desirous of presenting an erudite academic opus. I am grateful to have become an experienced practitioner in the arena, a "do leader," particularly given that my practice took me off the planet in command of a US human space mission.

I also believe exercising leadership in life or death team situations serves as a powerful, crystallizing influence for doing it right. It matters when you and the team could die if you mess up. If you do not execute, circumstances may conspire to execute you, in a very real sense. In that regard, the experiences of an astronaut leader parallel those of others, such as world-class mountain climbers. Yet they also differ in that so much of the activity in the astronaut preparation phase takes place in office and meeting settings, very much like your real-world place of business. For any troubadour author, that workplace team grounding is just as essential to his expertise as the life-or-death actions in the crucible of dynamic execution.

The Content Intent: Story Centered

With the troubadour outlook in mind, the intent here is to embed key principles within relevant examples and stories. I learned early in my speaking career the incredible power of story to affect others positively. Although we need to build our cases on the bedrock of facts and data, I've learned that we must also freely call on feelings and emotions to energize our examples. A story that hopes to influence and deeply impress others must also have a moral. What do we learn? How do we grow from having read or heard it? Accordingly, I resolved to minimize trips down any sort of memory lane just to reminisce. Only if a personal recollection could demonstrate universal relevance would it pass muster.

If you happen to be the kind of space enthusiast like the gentleman who contacted me after my first mission to inform me I was the 301ˢᵗ person to go into space and that the mission lasted exactly fourteen days, zero hours, twelve minutes, and thirty-two seconds, the relative paucity of space trivia here might disappoint you. This book is not one of spaceflight details. Sorry, but it has a different purpose. Its mission is for practical leadership and teamwork content to hitch a ride on the spaceship of my astronaut and space shuttle commander credentials and examples. There are plenty of the former type of book, many written by my astronaut colleagues. This work, in contrast, is the first specific teamwork and leadership business book that an astronaut, let alone a mission commander, has written.

I'd also add that I did not use a ghostwriter for one single paragraph of this book. I understand the value that teaming with a professional writer can bring to the enterprise of telling one's story, but felt that to present my unique space flyer leadership perspective, I shouldn't have a ghostwriter do the heavy lifting. I did, however, very much welcome help from professional editors.

In the story-crafting process, I found two types useful: vignettes and extended, detailed narratives, both extracted from my workplaces. That the particular story took place in the office, a cockpit, or floating around in space mattered less than how it tied to a specific aspect of teamwork and execution. Along the way, dozens of pertinent analogies kept coming to mind. One of the fun aspects of having learned all that esoteric rocket science stuff is making it more comprehensible and metaphorically useful to others. I promise, I've taken every one of those examples down to its essence without detailed technical discussion.

Stories form the backbone of this text. Nonetheless, it's vitally important to hang some nourishing meat on the bones! The meat, of course, is the content, those elements that you can use. In the development process, I had some concern that I might have gone slightly overboard with story after my sister Debbie, a very bottom-line-oriented banking executive, reviewed one of my chapters. She finished the lead story, set the draft down, and commented, "Rick, that's a fine story, but I want to know, right up front, what I'm going to get out of this chapter. How exactly will it help me and my team? What is the key concept that I have to apply? Spell it out quickly for me, even before you tell me any stories." Because of her no-nonsense approach to business and thirty-year career as a leader in the banking industry, I got her message loud and clear, and it drove the unit, chapter, and subsection layout.

The Subsystem of Chapter Structure

I strove from the start to find the right balance of detailed content and supporting stories. Each chapter absolutely needed a short, focused key concept: the Purposeful Performance Principle. Accordingly, after Debbie's feedback, I decided to state the principle right at the start of every chapter. It also made sense to incorporate a relevant inspiring quote to draw on the wisdom of others before launching off into the lead story of each chapter. Also, not every section of each chapter is primarily "story." About a third of them just dive right into the content, presenting the practices you and your team can employ.

Communicating with anyone from NASA, you run the risk of being inundated with acronyms. NASA even has acronyms for acronyms, and in a few deliciously ironic examples, they use acronyms longer than the words represented! I've attempted to minimize that behavior, but that ideal is not perfectly attainable. Whenever an acronym is used to propel a story, however, it is always spelled out first. More importantly, we've also created a few mnemonic devices and easy acronyms such as 4P, PAPA, STARS, MARS, EARTH, and NGC to help you remember important concepts. If I've gone to the trouble of turning an approach or framework into an acronym, I believe it is a crucial process and worth diligently following.

Chapter subsections expand on the particular applications of each leadoff principle. They bring forth different best practices, detailed explanations, and subtle nuances that tie into the overall guidance from that principle. Finally, I present the summary for each chapter as a "cue card." Cue cards in the orbiter cockpit cover critical steps in a given procedure and the immediately required actions astronauts must take in an emergency. They are slapped all over the flight deck, particularly for launch and reentry. Here, each chapter cue card begins by presenting the Purposeful Performance Principle in abbreviated terms, boldfaced. "The Boldface" in aviation emergency procedures consists of the most crucial immediate-action steps, the ones the crew absolutely must commit to memory. Boldface always contains two elements: action verb and object. The cue card then summarizes expected results and team benefits. The "Crew Notes for Business Execution" provide a summary countdown with just enough details to remind you how to apply the lessons from each subsection. Finally, for fun and as a memory aid, I've also included a very short spaceflight metaphor or example tied to the overall chapter theme. The cue card chapter summaries represent content boiled down to its essence without the supporting stories.

What this book definitely is not is a research paper. Initially, I thought that it might prove helpful to include one business case study per chapter from a company completely outside my own industry to mix it up and further enhance relevance. After all, most business books employ some variation on that theme. It seemed to me, though, that if I did not have a personal tie-in to the story, I should not use it. The book does contain some short, specific company examples gathered from direct conversations with my clients or in my own industry of aerospace. However, there's some personal connection in every single instance.

Teamwork and leadership concepts and content are universal. In keeping with Gordy's troubadour tradition and Dr. Covey's validating words, my particular experiences should help you boldly and purposefully go into the sector of the teamwork galaxy where execution rules. The spaceship we'll fly is built in the hangar of my astronaut, test pilot, fighter pilot, and Air Force officer background. Its systems and subsystems are chapters, subsections, and cue cards, framed with examples and crewed with content. So let's get suited up and head out to the launch pad to begin the countdown to execution leadership for better results!

PART I
PURPOSE: THE WHY

Purpose is the very essence of why we're pursuing our venture in the first place. For downstream execution success, teams must first wisely address such abstract concepts and requirements. A sense of purpose drives inspiration and encompasses the most compelling aspects of human motivation. Vision, end state, and mission all fold into purpose. Purpose powers real, meaningful leadership.

Thinking of purpose, we typically consider the grand strategic imperatives. Because this book targets tactical execution and there's a plethora of resources and expertise on the strategy of purpose, I've limited the upfront discussion. However, because purpose lays the foundation for eventual execution, we must never set it aside. Even during daily execution activities, we should constantly keep it in mind. Accordingly, I often circle back to the "why" aspects of purpose—even in the six chapters otherwise devoted to execution. All of the elements of defining purpose are important, but two action-oriented ones carry through from strategy to tactical execution most forcefully.

First, the conscious act of choosing to do the most difficult things you can imagine in pursuit of your purpose induces action in and of itself. Setting the bar very high drives the attitude toward execution right from the start. Such choices make it very clear that success will require much hard work.

Second, coupling a Choose the Hard attitude with a purpose that makes a positive difference for others will define a meaningful mission. A Mission that Matters is always one of service. I've observed that when presented properly, few aspects of a mission prove more compelling to people for taking action than when they can forget themselves while helping others.

To lead with a compelling purpose, model the way in Choosing the Hard and finding the Mission that Matters. Once your team comes on board, they will eagerly seek to do whatever it takes to fulfill a purpose larger than themselves.

CHOOSE THE HARD

"*Audaces fortuna juvat—Fortune favors the bold.*"
–**Virgil**, from *The Aeneid*

This phrase is also the motto of the "Bold Tigers," the US Air Force 391st Tactical Fighter Squadron (TFS), in which I served. It's now designated the 391st Fighter Squadron; in 1991, the Air Force changed from TFS to FS for all fighter squadrons.

Purposeful Performance Principle 12: Actively seeking and embracing difficult challenges gives powerful initial direction, informs the vision, and encourages the team.

Consciously choosing to go after the toughest challenges empowers the process of finding purpose that deeply inspires. Such a positive, courageous start will energize and enable those who accept the call. Great leaders are able not only to define a vision, but also to awaken

the courage within people to relish risk and difficulty for the sake of pursuing a purpose of great worth beyond themselves.

We Choose

President John F. Kennedy, in a speech at Rice University in September 1962, publicly challenged our nation to land men on the moon and return them safely by the end of the decade. America's sum total of human spaceflight experience at that point consisted of four flights, six orbits total, and barely ten people-hours in space. Contrast that to 168 people-hours each and every day of our largest seven-person crews aboard the space shuttle, and it appears paltry indeed. How could we do it, and furthermore, why would our president ask of us such a seemingly improbable, if not impossible, task?

President Kennedy's uplifting rationale:

> We choose to go to the moon in this decade and do the other things, not because they are easy, but because they are hard, because that goal will serve to organize and measure the best of our energies and skills, because that challenge is one that we are willing to accept.

He framed the challenge, set the bar 250,000 miles high, and turned that orb hanging in the sky into the toughest of targets. Our national team rose to that challenge. We accomplished unimaginably more in exploration, science, and technology development than if we had just continued to coast along without that formidable target before us. The Apollo Program fired our imaginations and touched generations, even evolving humankind's sense of self as we viewed, for the first time, our beautiful blue-and-green home planet from afar. The palpable example to our nation and the world continues to inspire the very best, even to this day.

That Vision Thing

Crafting a vision, that highest of concepts guiding a team, is a nearly universal best practice these days. Virtually all of the hundreds of client companies I've spoken to during the last decade have carefully developed vision statements. It has been very rewarding to interact with these organizations and to support, through my presentations, the positive changes they aim to produce.

By its very nature, vision is a long-term consideration of a desired future state. Short, focused, clear, and inspiring—all these qualities are important in articulating vision. This book won't dwell on these aspects. By and large, most companies get it already. However, without this foundation, execution will waver and falter. Furthermore, the vision statements that stand out as most compelling are the ones that are the most demanding and have the deepest purpose.

It's inherent in human nature to aspire to a better future state. We all find it tougher, however, to willingly put forth the grinding effort to get there. Those who courageously Choose the Hard in their vision undoubtedly accomplish the most. The highest achievement end state requires the deepest commitment.

Accepting the Challenge

Absolutely nothing is easy about human spaceflight. The energy required to accomplish it is mindboggling. The environment is forbidding and treacherous. The preparation never ends. For the flight crews, the vast volume of details to learn and master are daunting. Multiple lurking, dangerous "unknown unknowns," any one of which could scuttle the mission and kill the crew, make it one of the most difficult ventures humans can undertake. Successful human spaceflight requires life-and-death teamwork and leadership. The fact that devoted flight crew and ground support teams alike generally make it look easy can diminish our appreciation of how tough it truly is.

The most difficult technical thing I've ever done in my life was to reach the required pinnacle of readiness to climb aboard space shuttle *Columbia* as a rookie pilot astronaut (PLT). The duties of the front-right-seat PLT position make it technically the most demanding crew position in the most complex aerospace vehicle ever built. Fortunately, I was immersed in an incredible crew-support culture that collectively and intuitively valued accepting rigorous challenges. With my commander (CDR), Air Force Colonel John Blaha, mentoring and encouraging, that team culture pulled me along and made the key difference in readiness and my value to the team.

I determined from that experience to model and emphasize Choosing the Hard in future leadership opportunities and team settings. Later in my astronaut career, that leadership opportunity came when I was selected to command the STS-90 Neurolab mission on *Columbia*. Neurolab was the most complex science research human space mission ever flown. The ambitious NASA and international science teams charged with making it a useful, productive mission pulled out all the stops. They heaped our plate to overflowing with an aggressive and complicated suite of world-class, leading-edge life science experiments. Most had never even been attempted in space.

With five rookies out of a seven-astronaut crew on this mission and the unparalleled payload complexity, it proved essential that every crewmember accept, even embrace, the challenge. It made my job as the leader easier and leveraged our team effectiveness with everyone's eagerness always to pay the price in doing the hard things needed for success.

In my consulting and speaking, I've worked with companies in industries as wide-ranging as banking to pharmaceuticals to oil drilling. Though business details vary widely, the organizational challenges are all essentially the same. Most don't actually do rocket science, but they all nevertheless operate in today's dazzlingly complex world. None of them can afford not to embrace the most difficult demands that complexity levies. In that increasingly demanding environment, though typically not a matter of life and death, success or failure hinges on effective leadership in pursuing those consciously chosen challenges.

Why Take the Risk?

Indeed, why take any risk? Committing deeply to a difficult purpose is risky, whether or not you literally risk your life. What if success doesn't come? How can I really get excited about this new team or latest initiative? What if I'm disappointed yet again if my team or I as an individual fall short?

Valid doubts and concerns may hold you back from diving headlong after the toughest challenges. However, the very act of courageously making that commitment starts up the passion engine. As your team builds on the commitment, that engine will rev up into overdrive. The result will be results!

It is never enough solely to have a predefined purpose. Teams that work and rework purpose, while actively pushing the limits, invest fully in their mission. Gaining a firm understanding of the mission's value naturally drives a willingness to choose a difficult, potentially risky path toward mission accomplishment. In turn, the purposeful dedication will set high expectations and contribute to an adaptive, high-performing organization.

Pause for a Collective Courage Top Off

Pad 39B at Kennedy Space Center (KSC), Florida. Seven crewmates in orange "pumpkin suits" step off the "astrovan" on a quiet and sunny Florida spring morning in 1998. The heady organic odor of surrounding swamps mingles incongruously with the faintly industrial smell of the pad complex. The crew pauses next to the slumbering *Columbia*, like hobbits gazing up at J.R.R. Tolkien's dragon Smaug.

When a rocket on a launch pad is fueled up and the support structure pulled away, it sighs, groans, and occasionally hisses as if alive, yet asleep. When it is a winged orbiter plastered astride a tank filled with 1.6 million pounds of liquid hydrogen and oxygen, in turn coupled to two monstrous solid rocket boosters (SRBs), that rocket truly resembles a mythical dragon. She's ready to awaken, breathe fire, and fling herself off the perch.

As planned, this team of miniscule humans takes a couple of minutes just to be in the moment. While standing in the shadow of their dragon, gazing up, they each ponder the import of what they will do in just a few hours.

Where did this short team interlude come from? Why was it part of the timeline? What was the point? There was certainly no required technical reason. It was commander initiated, from a mentor who had been through the process twice before. I had felt the awe-inspiring, intangible teambuilding benefit of taking a brief pause in such a dramatic setting just before plunging into full-execution mode. I was determined that my crew have the same opportunity to briefly ponder, in that dramatic setting, the magnificence of the enterprise of which they were privileged to be a part.

Everyone needed to recognize the collective effort and courage that had brought us together to this point. It would be a treasured memory for a lifetime.

With that thought in mind, I, as commander, insisted our schedulers build that five-minute pause into our tightly scheduled prelaunch timeline.

Personally, I considered how grateful I was to go to space again. As commander, I especially felt gratified to bring along a fully prepared team, including five rookies who had proven themselves. They were as ready and deserving as any astronauts ever to take that ride. Collectively, that joint experience topped off our personal courage propellant tanks. It was helpful to have that boost so close to the upcoming thunderous launch.

As empowering as courageously choosing difficult challenges can be, doing the hard work to get there can prove exhausting. The occasional pause to refresh and renew is valuable. Stepping back to ponder and reflect on the mission prepares everyone to serve more effectively.

A Mach-25 Commute Is Still Just a Commute

The variety and scope of missions flown on the space shuttle over thirty years is breathtaking, but not widely appreciated. This public perception is perhaps a natural consequence of so many flights, 135 in all, and because every launch and landing looks pretty similar. The payload purposes are fulfilled in orbit, mostly out of sight and mind to the casual observer. However, this unseen phase is the one that really matters.

Over the course of the program, these specialized missions fulfilled a plethora of deep and important purposes. The scientific and exploration accomplishments have indeed been profound. Launch and landing, though risky and exciting while moving along at up to twenty-five times the speed of sound, were really just the commute to and from that important payload work.

Because of the danger and difficulty, it would appear that preparing for the risky, dynamic launch and landing phases serve as prime examples of challenging purpose. However, when viewed in another light, those operations really just support the actual mission. It is important to recognize the true mission purpose and choose to stay focused on it. The challenge is to not allow yourself to be sidetracked from the ultimate purpose.

Any venture has its own "commute." Many team activities, sometimes even the urgent or exciting ones, don't contribute fully to the team purpose. We must constantly sort through all our activities and prioritize to promote those that give real payoff, or payload if you will.

Tough Targets

Sometimes the tough targets can be literal ones. Early in my Air Force career, I flew the F-111 Aardvark, a specialized, swing-wing, low-level, all-weather night attack aircraft. The Vark was the fastest airplane in the world at sea level altitudes. My teammates and I at RAF Lakenheath, England, trained daily against incredibly tough targets; we're talking little footbridges across meandering streams in the glens of the Scottish Highlands.

As a pilot, I teamed up with my Weapons Systems Officer (WSO) to navigate at treetop level to these training targets at over six hundred miles per hour, sometimes faster, often in dense fog and clouds. We'd find the target via radar, infrared sensors, or the Mark One Eyeball. Then we would track it and run a simulated attack, all within just a few seconds of the appointed time. Onboard mission tapes and bombing scores from the range, reviewed in a comprehensive debriefing after every mission, measured how we did.

The payoff? Operation El Dorado Canyon. President Reagan ordered this attack in 1986 to respond to Libyan leader Muammar Gaddafi's support of terrorist attacks in Germany. In the dark at 2:00 a.m. local time, April 15, 1986, eighteen Lakenheath F-111s streaked inbound at low level, nearly supersonic over the Mediterranean Sea, and obliterated the assigned targets in Tripoli and the Benghazi Airfield. When he saw how huge his target was as it filled his infrared scope, the Benghazi lead WSO loudly exclaimed for the mission tape, "Ooh, baby!" What a contrast to the tiny, hard-to-find practice targets. Choosing the tough targets in training had paid off well.

I had rotated back stateside to Mountain Home Air Force Base, Idaho in 1984 to become an instructor pilot and train new F-111 crewmembers in the 391st Tactical Fighter Squadron (TFS), the "Bold Tigers." Like other stateside-stationed Aardvark drivers, I missed this particular operation. A third of the world away, I had range control officer duty that same day at Saylor Creek Bombing Range in southern Idaho. Two F-111s checked in on the radio and asked me if I'd heard what our Lakenheath buddies had done. I hadn't, so the lead pilot told me, "They just went and clobbered Gaddafi!" I responded, "And we're here bombing Idaho. You're cleared hot!" We were incredibly proud of our colleagues when we learned the details of the mission. Although disappointed in not being able to be there for the action ourselves, we honored them. We also appreciated that through disciplined adherence to choosing tough targets, they were ready when the nation called.

The aspect of honoring comrades after Operation El Dorado Canyon also manifested a more personal and poignant tone. I learned a day after the raid that one of my former WSOs, Captain Paul Lorence, was killed during the attack. I had been his first aircraft commander in the 492nd TFS, the "Madhatters." This brilliant, likable, and courageous gentleman and I had gone after many of those little Scottish footbridges together. It takes courage to pay the required price when Choosing the Hard. In Paul's case, it was the ultimate price.

The experience from Operation El Dorado Canyon, coupled with continued, disciplined training, further prepared the F-111 community for more action a few years later. Using the Pave Tack precision-guided weapons system, F-111s in Desert Storm turned in a stellar performance against a full range of ground targets. They destroyed more enemy aircraft than any other warplane, made over fifteen hundred verified armor kills, and delivered the special heavyweight bunker-buster, laser-guided bombs that finally convinced Saddam he had no place to hide.

Max Q: Push on Through

Max Q is a fairly well-known term from space shuttle operations. Because the NASA public affairs announcers always pointed out when the launching shuttle encountered max Q, I meet many people who've heard of it. Perhaps because it sounds cool and spacey, they also tend to remember the term, even though they might not know exactly what it is. Max Q describes the point of maximum aerodynamic stress on an aircraft or launching rocket as it speeds through the atmosphere.

The amount of Q, or dynamic pressure, comes from two sources: the thickness of the air the vehicle is passing through and the vehicle's speed. The actual formula is $\frac{1}{2}$ *rho* V^2, where the Greek letter *rho* is the air's density and

V^2 is the true airspeed squared. Squaring the speed very quickly drives up the dynamic pressure and stress as we accelerate. This concept directly ties to the idea of Choosing the Hard and, in particular, choosing to counter the resistance and difficulties that come along as we pick up steam in our execution.

When we go after the most challenging goals to fulfill our purpose, we must, with open eyes, realize from the start that we will meet all kinds of resistance. Opposition will be present in all things—that's the inherent nature of moving to a better state. The thicker the air, the greater the resistance. One way to handle that resistance is, like the space shuttle, to focus on traveling a quickly ascending path. Because in the atmosphere the air density drops off rapidly with altitude, a launching rocket stays close to vertical until climbing above most of the atmosphere, then really ramps up the speed to continue to orbit. For us, upon making our choices and recognizing the opposition, we must concentrate on staying above the fray of the lesser distractions and more petty concerns. Diligent focus on our purpose is necessary. Before we know it, many of those high-density resistance items have fallen behind us, and we're on our way.

The velocity squared aspect of max Q further extends the metaphor. The F-111, because of its high speed at very low altitudes, generated much more dynamic pressure than the space shuttle. The shuttle, being very blunt and "draggy," needed to get up and out of the atmosphere before it could really reach its incredible speed. If it went much faster than the limit of 420 knots "indicated airspeed" (directly related to dynamic pressure), the orbiter nose structure would cave in. The F-111, though, was very sleek with low drag. I once saw 848 knots of indicated airspeed in level flight at sea level—nearly one thousand miles per hour. That's a max Q of over four times that of the space shuttle! No problem, though; the sleek, low-drag design reduced the forces on the structure and made operating at such high dynamic pressure an everyday thing.

The lesson for us in Choosing the Hard is to look concurrently for every opportunity to reduce the drag. The solution must never be to reduce the speed or energy with which we pursue the difficult. The drive for pace and energy is an inherent requirement for successful achievement in a Choose the Hard approach. However, it's also vitally important when consciously accelerating on a challenging path to wisely consider how to make our operations efficient, streamlined, and effective. Those detailed considerations come out less here than in the execution techniques and approaches described later as part of the PAPA model. Suffice it to say that, in terms of purpose, we need to launch with a firm commitment to generate the necessary speed and energy, while recognizing that we will have to overcome much high Q resistance on the way to success.

Energizing the Team

Is the potential of your team fully tapped? A team needs deeper inspiration than that which comes from just working the daily tasks. A well-defined purpose for team existence and work is fundamental to unleashing that potential in a productive way. Furthermore, a purpose that requires the most stretching will call forth the most focused, productive effort. A central guiding, meaningful purpose will establish key priorities. With those priorities clearly understood, a team can then integrate all activities for productive accomplishment.

But what about buy-in? A team may have a purpose defined for it and the team members might clearly understand what is expected, but if they haven't internalized the purpose, it will not prove effective in mission accomplishment. Effective teams need to have everyone on board in pursuing their common purpose.

Although essentially a leadership role to initiate the excitement to drive that internalization, it is a cascading leadership responsibility. In other words, everyone on the team can and should exercise the influence to help generate and sustain that energy. Involving the team from the start in establishing challenging purpose generates far more momentum than if it just comes down from the top.

Choosing the Hard provides the courage to get out to the launch pad. Furthermore, making the emotional effort to energize people to make such choices will ignite the fire that lifts them off the pad.

Support and Encouragement for the Choosers of the Hard

Reassurance and assistance should come from all quarters in team ventures. In the space-flying business, families and friends make a huge difference. They really are just as important a part of our mission support team as anyone else.

Two minutes prior to my first launch, atop the Launch Control Complex (LCC), my wife Julie waited anxiously with other family members, including Chief Astronaut Robert "Hoot" Gibson. Rhea Seddon, Hoot's wife, was my crewmate, sitting on the pad with me. With the countdown clock drawing down, Julie leaned over to my boss and asked, "Hoot, what's harder, being out there or being here?" Immediately and unequivocally, speaking as the supportive spouse, he replied, "Oh, it's much harder standing here," as he waited in suspense for Rhea to take that fiery ride. The brave astronaut, test pilot, and combat fighter pilot was just as courageous in that support role as in any of his legendary flying accomplishments.

In supporting my dream, Julie exercised her own quiet, profound courage. She recognized that, as a couple, we were engaged in an amazing venture with overarching and significant purpose. The message for all of us: exercise the daily courage to support our teammates and our nearest and dearest in their tough assignments and challenges. Be there for them. That willingness to support often requires just as difficult a choice as climbing aboard a space shuttle.

The Common Thread: Courage to Try

Early in a team's life cycle, team members must lay the foundation for the team's existence and work. This forming stage requires high-level, conceptual considerations of vision and mission. Making the active choice to follow the challenging path will encouragingly bind the team to vision and mission. Internalizing such an approach strengthens any team.

Making the conscious choice to attempt difficult things takes courage. It may or may not require physical courage, but it always takes moral courage. Sometimes that moral courage requires performing a single disagreeable task that you dread, like letting a nice but nonperforming employee go. Most often, however, the gritty determination to embrace tough challenges daily will help you overcome whatever specific problems you and your team face. While it takes discipline and a measure of courage to Choose the Hard consistently, the very mindset itself is incredibly empowering. Facing challenges squarely creates a virtuous, positive cycle, building more strength to face each succeeding challenge.

People occasionally query astronauts about how they find the courage to strap into a rocket: "You mean you actually want to ride that low bidder-built contraption?" We've all spent most of a lifetime dreaming of going to space, choosing to study and work in the most challenging technical disciplines and joining teams of likeminded individuals. After that, we don't generally consider ourselves as particularly courageous to climb aboard and go. It's just what we do. Most of the courage that is involved is in the determination to choose a difficult path and then stick to it. Furthermore, fervently believing that what you are doing is manifestly important makes that kind of courage easy to exercise.

Stretching to your visionary, desired future state and executing to fulfill your mission absolutely requires a courageous mentality. Choose the Hard, intentionally, actively, boldly. Such boldness is your team's own "astrovan." It will provide the motivating force to head out to the launch pad in the first place, climb aboard, and strap in for the wild ride to come.

—CUE CARD—

CHOOSE THE HARD

> ### *ACTIVELY SEEK AND ACCEPT*
> ### *DIFFICULT CHALLENGES*

Result: Choosing the Hard produces a powerful start, informs the vision, and sets the team up for greater achievement.

Team Benefit: Accepting difficult challenges encourages and inspires the team from the start.

Crew Notes for Business Execution:

10	Choosing the Hard serves to "organize and measure the best of our energies and skills."
9	The highest-achievement, visionary end state calls for the greatest commitment.
8	Success in today's complex, very competitive business environment requires the conscious choice to embark on difficult paths.
7	Embrace the emotional risks of enthusiastically and fully committing to the meaningful team purpose.
6	Regularly pausing to reflect on mission challenges will spur on the team.
5	Avoid excessive time on activities that, though urgent or exciting, don't support the main purpose of the team.
4	Choosing the Hard takes sacrifice, but it is for a greater good.
3	Generate energized buy-in through involving the team from the start in establishing a challenging and definite purpose.
2	Providing daily support and encouragement sustains the entire team.
1	Proactively and boldly Choosing the Hard takes courage and gives courage.

Spaceflight Metaphor: Choosing the Hard gives the courage to head out to the launch pad and strap in.

MAKE THE
MISSION MATTER

"There is no passion to be found playing small—in settling for a life that is less than the one you are capable of living."
—Nelson Mandela

Purposeful Performance Principle 11: A meaningful cause in service to others inspires team members to fully commit to mission accomplishment.

A Mission that Matters, one of service that helps others, strengthens the team-binding power of attempting to conquer difficult challenges. Teams not only need to be good, they need to be good for something. Furthermore, individuals respond to the inspiration of serving a cause greater than themselves. The best leaders

incorporate that response into an organization that truly will make a positive difference for customers and stakeholders.

Cheerful Dedication

Somewhere over planet Earth, another sixteen-hour orbit workday winds down. As the pilot, I'm busy on the flight deck, running the imaginatively (not) named "Pre-Sleep Activity" checklist. It's a mundane routine to get ready to bed down for the night. Just like at home, it requires setting the alarm for the next day's wakeup, but it also includes slightly more esoteric tasks, like repositioning *Columbia*'s external dish antenna and reconfiguring cryogenic hydrogen and oxygen tank heaters.

All of a sudden, ecstatic giggling and guffaws peal out from the middeck, interrupting the quiet hum of the ventilation fans. I think, *Must be a great joke. I've got to check it out.* I float headfirst through the inter-deck access. John Blaha and Shannon Lucid are doubled over in joyous laughter in the middeck. The view reminds me of the scene in *Mary Poppins* where everyone giggles his or her way to the ceiling. No special effects here, though—my laughing colleagues really are floating.

"What's so funny, guys? Let me in on it." John, through his ear-to-ear grin, exclaims, "Rick, do you realize that WE ARE IN SPACE?" Playing the straight man, I nod and say, "Well, uh, yes, John, I just saw Earth way down below, so I figure we're in space all right."

"It's the greatest thing ever! Being in space, WOW!" John, veteran but never jaded, always zestfully wears his passion for space on his sleeve. Teamed up with Shannon, the epitome of the word cheerful, they're a spontaneous laughter rocket, just waiting to blast off at any time: energetic, ecstatic, and enthusiastic.

Coupled with that passion, John and Shannon deeply believed in our work. They were fully vested, intellectually and emotionally, and were purposeful, consummate professionals like every other crewmate on my three flights. When required, they were as serious and focused as anyone I've ever met. As commander, John's every leadership effort and all his guiding advice concentrated on accomplishing the mission. Shannon, like all the rest of us on the crew, similarly modeled commitment to the core.

What a remarkable combination: having a deep purpose that you take very seriously, yet cheerfully, even gleefully, not taking yourself too seriously. Finding a meaningful purpose will deeply inspire anyone. Enthusiastically acting on the purpose will take it to the next level and invigorate your entire team.

The Mission That Matters: Service to Others

Gravity affects virtually every physiological function. No earth-based life evolved without it. Even after more than fifty years of humans flying in space, we still understand, at a detailed scientific level, relatively little about how life responds in gravity's absence. Long-term, for continued human space exploration and eventual settlement, a more comprehensive understanding is absolutely crucial.

The overall purpose of my third spaceflight, STS-90 Neurolab on *Columbia*, was "to go to outer space to explore inner space." That exploration was fundamental research. As a crew, preparing to risk our lives flying this mission, we knew that the work was important. As commander, with overall responsibility for safe and effective mission execution, I constantly contemplated its meaningful purpose. We considered our labor as essential prep work to support a compelling, long-term vision of expanding human presence off the home planet. Broadly speaking, it was service to humankind.

More inspiring for me were the potential benefits for all humans, not just astronauts. Space-based life science research holds great promise for all of us down on the planet. Many of the deficits and phenomena that occur in healthy, relatively young astronauts in weightlessness mirror certain earthbound disease processes and injuries. Accordingly, the space neuroscience of STS-90 offered significant potential to add to the understanding of conditions like stroke, traumatic brain injury, neuropathy, and so forth. The potential to serve individual people here on Earth with debilitating health concerns—not just a nebulous future humankind—is a Mission that Matters.

Every team needs a Mission that Matters. The good news is that, in most business operations today, the core opportunity for service is already in place. Beyond returning value to shareholders, it is likely your company could not exist if it couldn't provide a service of worth to a bigger audience. You do not even need to be part of a company in an inherent service business. It's easy to see that the mission for a cutting-edge research and development pharmaceutical company creating new ways to treat cancer inherently matters. However, regardless of how mundane any other business may seem in comparison, thoughtful consideration can also lead to a meaningful, service-oriented mission.

The question becomes, "How do we recognize the deeper service prerogative for our team?" The required orientation is fundamentally about developing a sincere desire to exercise stewardship, which is important but not natural to most people. Stewardship requires a careful and responsible approach to giving meaningful service to others. It takes keen awareness and practice, and is a difficult path to choose.

Once mission is found and elucidated, the team needs to keep it top of mind, even while executing daily. Pressing to reach short-term sales targets or quarterly bottom-line performance metrics, for example, should not squeeze out a team's mindfulness of the deeper benefit to others they provide.

Should your team members awake every single morning, look in the mirror, and say to themselves, "Today I'm going to work because our mission matters, and I'll be serving others"? Of course not—let's be real. However, when the concept is ingrained, it informs all that the team does. An authentic, empathetic, "What can I do for you?" attitude will operate within the team itself to the benefit of culture and productivity. A service-before-self mindset developed internally will manifest itself externally in positive customer and stakeholder relationships.

Having a mission that truly matters requires service to others. Teams should frame the mission with that in mind. Even though doing so is challenging, teams that bend their planning and efforts toward service will prove more inspired and, ultimately, more effective.

Fly It; Live It

In 1997, I received word I would command the STS-90 Neurolab flight, focused exclusively on researching the effects of weightlessness on the brain and nervous system. With a technical background in aeronautical engineering and fluid physics, I'm certainly no life scientist or medical doctor, but space shuttle mission command is reserved for experienced pilot astronauts.

As a pilot astronaut, being assigned to command the pure-research mission STS-90 presented an attitudinal fork in the road. I, PLT Scott Altman, and flight engineer (MS2) Kay Hire, with absolutely no negative feedback from NASA management, could have focused exclusively on our own technical roles. After all, we had a full plate in learning how to take *Columbia* to and from space and keep her running well while there. It was important, however, to ask ourselves whether we should align solely with launch, entry, and vehicle systems' tasks in orbit, or whether we should immerse ourselves in the payload too.

Knowing from my previous space flights how gratifying it is to be embedded in mission purpose, I counseled my two rookie flight-deck crewmates that we should take the deepest dive possible into the Neurolab science world. These teammates responded spectacularly as we worked with our scientist astronauts, Rick Linnehan, Dave Williams, Jay Buckey, and Jim Pawelczyk (all docs —lots of letters like PhD, MD, and DVM after their names) to plan and prepare in a way that would maximize the science return.

CDR, PLT, MS2, with military aviation backgrounds but without years of experience in the medical field, often just acted as test subjects or technicians in the Spacelab module. When our own duties permitted, our voluntary payload engagement freed up "doc time" for what only a doc could do, coalesced the team around our common purpose, and inspired a genuine and unanimous passion for the "why" of this particular flight. Together, we all "went to outer space to explore inner space."

The highly successful STS-90 Neurolab mission is the only space shuttle flight ever to have had a book published of peer-reviewed, "out-of-this-world" science papers. In that sense, it's one of the most productive human space missions ever flown. Was commitment to that purpose worth a small but nontrivial risk of dying to accomplish it? Unquestionably, passionately, yes!

Ignition . . . and . . . Liftoff!

T minus two minutes—down comes the visor. You hear the swooshing "whoo, whoo" of your own breathing just as if you've entered the action with Astronaut Dave Bowman in the movie *2001: A Space Odyssey*. At T-2:01, you're part of a little community of four on the flight deck. You speak directly with one another as necessary and, at times, with a lighthearted comment to keep things loose. At T-1:59, you're alone with your thoughts, communicating only via the electronic intercom with your crewmates just a couple feet away. Reaching that milestone always signaled to me the reality of what I was about to do.

The last few minutes of a launch countdown are simultaneously thrilling and nerve racking. With each passing event during the count, you know you're getting closer to springing off the pad. For the CDR and PLT, though, you also visualize everything you might have to do should something go wrong during ascent. It's stimulating, with adrenaline building to just the right level to give optimum performance. I have never felt so alive or at the peak of my potential.

Energized? Oh, yes! Deeply committed to the mission? By definition, you're committed—you're strapped in, willingly, at the pointy end of a vehicle filled with millions of pounds of highly volatile propellants! You've worked tirelessly to prepare, had the courage to head to the launch pad, and now are eager to go.

On all three of my launches, at some point within those last two minutes, a few thoughts would come to mind along the lines of, *I can't believe I'm here. What a privilege. This mission really matters. Now, don't screw anything up!* The firm commitment as a team member to become one with the mission purpose naturally rose to the top of my thoughts in that anticipation-filled timeframe.

Every time I sat on the launch pad, I deeply appreciated the fact that I was about to embark not just on an incredible adventure, but on an important venture. Any undertaking hoping for success must have an important and meaningful purpose behind it. As you and your teams have chosen to pursue difficult challenges, you've courageously made it to your own launch pads. Then, after deliberately and thoughtfully defining a meaningful purpose, your team too can ignite the boosters to leap off that pad into purposeful action.

No Wheel Spinning, a Caution

Passion is overrated. At least, shallow fervor without focus and deep, abiding commitment is often far overvalued. Have you ever worked with excited, well-intentioned people who nevertheless just seem to keep running around in circles? You can call that behavior, to borrow a term from military aviation, "high PRF." PRF is the pulse repetition frequency of a radar. In high-PRF mode, a radar is pinging away faster than you can follow, just like the frenetic pace of the high-energy person who is not purposeful.

I've observed individuals in many organizations, from squadrons to corporations, who constantly flit from one "bright, shiny object" to another. In particular, one midlevel officer in one of my squadrons was definitely an energetic, even passionate person, but we junior officers always felt like we were out on the end of the rope as we were required to play crack the whip. We continually discussed among ourselves how he could never seem to get out of high-PRF mode. It was difficult to get much of anything done. We saw firsthand that the endless tasking on peripheral projects detracted from our ability to prepare for the actual mission. Execution was weaker than it needed to be. The sense of purpose definitely suffered.

Regardless of the energy level, unfocused performance is not purposeful and will not accomplish the mission. Both components, high energy and focused pursuit of a definite purpose, must exist and stay balanced within the team. Everyone needs to understand the central purpose of the team and, with that understanding, spawn a productive passion for fulfilling it. Do not ever mistake activity for progress. All airspeed and no direction just gets you lost. Drive the enthusiasm toward the actual purpose and you'll see real results.

Contagious Enthusiasm: The KidSat Payload

Astronauts sit through hundreds of briefings during mission training. Of all the myriad of payload briefings I ever heard, though, a group of high school kids from La Cañada Flintridge, California, presented the absolute best. Why were high school kids briefing an astronaut crew? These students were working on "KidSat," an add-on flight deck experiment for my second mission, STS-76 on *Atlantis*. This experiment was part of NASA's educational outreach efforts, officially a very low-priority payload.

KidSat consisted of an electronic still camera mounted in an overhead window. With *Atlantis* flipped upside down relative to Earth, the camera, controlled through a laptop computer and uplinks from the ground, snapped photos of selected ground sites. Active during our sleep period, it was supposed to be a set-up-and-forget operation. If any problems arose, we were not to spend much time trying to fix them. Scientists at NASA's Jet Propulsion Laboratory in California managed the project, but the high school students who briefed us had written the controlling software. This software enabled selected middle school students nationwide to operate the electronic still camera remotely via the communications uplinks and downlinks.

These very bright kids briefing us brought boundless energy and amazing passion to the KidSat project. Their attitudes astounded us in their intensity and conviction. The students did not realize it, but they were exercising powerful influence and leadership with that purposeful enthusiasm. Our entire six-astronaut crew vowed that, regardless of its official status as a low-priority payload, we would absolutely do whatever it took on our end to make sure it worked.

Enthusiastic, deep caring within a team or project is contagious. While fortune favors the bold, it particularly smiles on the boldly passionate! By the way, the payload operated flawlessly, captured great images, and proved a powerful educational tool as it directly connected students all over North America to the wonders and educational value of seeing the Earth from space.

"Light This Candle!"

Astronaut Alan Shepard, America's first man in space, was, according to his biographer Neal Thompson in *Light This Candle: The Life and Times of Alan Shepard*, a "complicated and conflicted man . . . somewhat of an enigma." Alternately showing up as the "Ice Commander" or "Smilin' Al," he had a reputation for being rather moody. Unlike some of his original Mercury colleagues, he certainly was not outgoing with the press or public. Shepard typically maintained a distance and reserve, perhaps reflective of his stoic New England upbringing.

Yet underneath the protective veneer, Shepard carried an unparalleled dedication to mission purpose. Thompson describes him as a "very intense guy who just wanted to get the job done and move forward and not look back." Sitting on the pad in his tiny capsule during a frustrating technical delay on May 5, 1961, that intensity and mission focus came out. Shepard's famous chiding of the launch team became the stuff of legends when he pointedly asked, "Why don't you fix your little problem and light this candle?"

A deeper and longer-term dedication to purpose arose later, when Shepard was medically grounded with a vertigo-inducing inner-ear condition known as Meniere's disease. Rather than depart NASA and capitalize on any of a number of lucrative offers, purpose drove him in 1963 to take a lower profile, yet instrumental, role as the head of the Astronaut Office. Eventually, the medical condition was resolved, and Shepard commanded Apollo 14 and walked on the moon. He served in the Astronaut Corps for fifteen years—always steadfastly, though not necessarily gregariously, committed to NASA's purpose.

My direct connection to Alan Shepard was limited to a very brief meeting at the 1990 Astronaut Reunion when I was a brand-new astronaut trainee. Yet perhaps because I grew up in New Hampshire also, just a few miles away from Admiral Shepard's hometown, I always viewed him as a superb professional role model. In fact, after Shepard and teacher-in-space Christa McAuliffe, of the ill-fated *Challenger* mission, I became the third person from New Hampshire to set course for space.

Following in such footsteps approaching my first launch, I felt a great responsibility to perform my duties well and fulfill the mission purpose. You just can't let down those who have trodden that path before, the role models whose purposeful passion, however expressed, helped you along the way.

Aspirational Vigor

Early August 1998, just a few months after STS-90, I'm sitting at my desk in the Astronaut Office. An email query from NASA Aircraft Ops pops up on my computer screen: "We need pilot volunteers to fly the four-ship T-38 missing man formation flyby for Admiral Shepard's memorial service at JSC [Johnson Space Center, in Houston, where the astronauts are based]" The two-place T-38 Talon is the zippy little white-and-blue supersonic jet we astronauts have flown since the sixties for official transport, to maintain our flying proficiency and, from time to time, to memorialize our colleagues who have passed on. Admiral Shepard had passed away peacefully at home from leukemia on July 21st, twenty-nine years to the day from when the Apollo 11 lunar module *Eagle* lifted off the surface of the moon to return to Earth.

I typed a response as quickly as I could and then followed up with a phone call: "I'm in, absolutely. Don't even think about not including me. And I need to fly as number three" (the position of the missing man who would pull up and out of formation as it passed overhead). During the flyby, after concentrating to stay tucked in tightly in close formation three feet away from the lead aircraft, I feel a deep and poignant reverence as I make the abrupt pull up and steep afterburner climb out of sight to represent the "missing man."

That certainly was one of the emotional highlights of all my years in the Astronaut Corps. The feeling of that day was further reinforced a few weeks later when I received a very kind handwritten thank-you note from Admiral Shepard's daughter, Laura Shepard Churchley. I was then able to connect with her and, as the third New Hampshire astronaut, express my gratitude for what her father had represented to me. What a privilege to help pay tribute to a fellow Granite Stater and honor a boyhood hero, one whose dedication prompted me to aspire with vigor after a purpose greater than myself.

Whether mission commitment manifests itself in the long-term dedication of a hero and legend whose still waters run deep or in the vibrant, youthful exuberance of high-school kids, it contains power to influence and inspire all team members. A team with a healthy, positive, mission-oriented culture generates aspirational vigor. Vigor implies strength and health; aspirational implies growing and stretching. Meaningful purpose drives that healthy, energetic stretching and infuses the team with power to go get the job done. Execution is, after all, about doing, and energetic, inspired people accomplish far more of value than those passive, uncommitted souls who can't ever seem to make things happen.

—CUE CARD—

MAKE THE MISSION MATTER

REINFORCE ENTHUSIASTICALLY
MEANINGFUL MISSION OF SERVICE TO OTHERS

Result: A meaningful mission drives deep commitment to executing well.

Team Benefit: A mission that matters of service to others energizes and focuses team members.

Crew Notes for Business Execution:

8	Take your mission very seriously, but not yourself.
7	A Mission that Matters requires service to others.
6	Step out of individual comfort zones and expertise areas to expand your ability to contribute to the overall team effort.
5	Seek meaningfulness. Turn your adventures into ventures and vice versa.
4	Couple high energy with focused performance. Both are required for effective execution.
3	Enthusiasm is contagious. Fortune doubly smiles on the boldly passionate.
2	Passion is really a reflection of intense commitment. It can run quiet and deep, just as well as loud and animated.
1	Purpose-derived passion gives a team powerful aspirational vigor to energetically get the work done and accomplish the mission.

Spaceflight Metaphor: Purpose with passion lights the fire to launch the team on their way.

PART II
PEOPLE: THE WHO

People comprise the most crucial component of the 4P model. In a team, people compensate for both high-level conceptual shortfalls and the devil-in-the details operational errors. Somehow, even when lacking clear initial direction and facing imposing daily operational barriers, teams with the right people make it through, often far better than you might expect. All of us need to pay attention to building the multitude of intangible people aspects within the team at every opportunity. Though not the teamwork per se, teambuilding with the people side is essential. While the infinite variety of people-related team aspects could fill volumes, here I've chosen to focus on two key aspects: building the team interrelationships and the preeminent need for trust within the team. Both these aspects reinforce people's ability to actively pursue meaningful purpose.

Leaders should see their role as the prime enabler for the people in their organization to get the work done that will fulfill the mission. Execution leadership is about making sure the right things are accomplished. Leaders enable that when they strengthen the interrelationships between team members and build up and train the team members themselves. I call this process Working the Matrix. The matrix consists of nodes (the individuals) all connected through the links (the interrelationships). When the matrix is whole and strong, the team can act together to do the right things that lead to excellent execution.

Closely related to building and strengthening the team matrix is the firm requirement for trust infused throughout every relationship internal to the team and external with other stakeholders. Trust is unquestionably a first-order necessity for teams to execute their missions at the highest levels. It is built on an even more fundamental basis, a zeroth-order prerequisite of trustworthiness of each team member. More than any other quality, leaders must demonstrate unflinching integrity and competence to model that trustworthiness. If they do, they will be able to lead through virtually any other challenge the team faces when operating. It's an absolute execution imperative.

It would take many books to address all the powerful concepts of the people side of a venture. When it comes to execution, though, the broad shepherding of relationships, coupled with a deep level of trust, will enable the team members to act consistently in alignment with their deepest values in pursuit of the highest purpose.

 **10**

WORK THE MATRIX

"I'm trying to free your mind, Neo. But I can only show you the door. You're the one that has to walk through it."
— **Morpheus**, in *The Matrix*

Purposeful Performance Principle 10: Constant care of the matrix of both internal and external relationships amplifies team unity and leverages effective collaboration.

W e should conceptualize our team and outside stakeholder groups each as a matrix of nodes of individual people connected through linking relationships. Every individual within each matrix is of incredible worth and deserves the utmost in development. Leaders must keep at the forefront of their minds the constant need to nourish and reinforce the connections. Links and nodes together, if strong, produce cohesion and unity directed toward a purposeful mission.

What's a Leader's Real Job?

It was late on a Friday afternoon, and I was deep into the training flow for my first mission, STS-58. I worked feverishly to wrap up another long week so that I could go home to tuck my daughters into bed.

Commander John Blaha and I were the last two crewmembers at work. Just as I prepared to head out, John asked, "Rick, what do you think my job is?" *That's easy*, I thought. "Well, John," I said, "you're the boss. You take care of life support and the computers, and you'll land *Columbia* when we come home."

"All true, but my real job is to work the matrix." I hadn't read anything in the stacks of training manuals about any matrix! "OK, John, I'll bite. What are you talking about?"

"The matrix is the seven by seven set of relationships among all of us on the crew. I absolutely must work that matrix carefully to build the crew. Then when we get to orbit and inevitably some things go wrong, all seven of us will pull together to solve the problems and have a successful mission." He explained that until you've been there, it's impossible to fully appreciate the unique difficulties of operating effectively in the weightless environment.

John knew that absolute team cohesion would make the critical difference. The deep conversation on teamwork that ensued profoundly enlightened me. It also strengthened my already deep respect for this great mentor's leadership skills. During the remaining months until launch, I made certain to save some brain space for leadership learning, even while cramming all the technical material into my head. I watched John carefully as he continued, steadily and purposefully, to develop the team. This rookie pilot was striving to be an effective crewmember in the technically most challenging space shuttle crew position, but I also enjoyed the privilege of learning from a masterful team builder at work, sensitized to the criticality of what he was doing. From that day I've always striven to work the matrix with every team of which I am part.

When I arrived home, it was well past the girls' bedtimes, but that night I didn't regret having missed the stories, hugs, and prayers. Why? Because I had gained an invaluable insight and approach that would stick with me forever in all my future team, and even family, interactions.

Building Nodes: Developing Individual Team Members

Individual team members are the nodes within the matrix. Four key aspects of building up individual team members require everyone be respected, recognized, strengthened, and trained. It's easy to keep these elements in mind with their alphabetical flow: double R, S, and T.

Typically, the designated leader or parent organization provides some formal means of applying these principles. Most companies have one or more established award programs. A well-defined and administered recognition program will honor those who perform over and above the norm.

Sometimes even government regulatory agencies mandate important standards in these areas. For example, the amazing overall safety record of modern commercial aviation reflects stringent Federal Aviation Administration crew-training requirements. Legislation mandating core levels of respect for individual dignity and safety are also vitally important. These formal means, whether required or best practices driven, are, with very few exceptions, already in place in today's business world.

Even with formal means of offering respect, recognition, strengthening, and training, in a refined team culture, all team members will regularly act informally on each of these four elements. Without defined requirements, you have to constantly pay attention to these numerous, small, node-building opportunities. Keep your radar scanning! Think of the times when you've been the beneficiary when fellow team members showed you respect, offered a pat on the back for a job well done, provided the encouraging word on a down day, or shared a few tips and techniques to help you do your job more effectively. Likewise, remember the occasions where you, subtly or overtly, built the nodes within your matrix.

We've already seen how a rookie astronaut was the fortunate beneficiary of some superlative informal leadership training through a commander's wisdom. Subsequent chapters will further discuss other formal aspects of training and preparation in building team competence. In considering a few more examples, please ponder the daily chances you have to offer team members these informal reinforcements. Building nodes helps create powerful teams. It's a vital leadership skill—not just for the official, designated leader, but for everyone.

Respect: A Nearly Surreal Experience

In 1977, as a twenty-one-year-old US Air Force Academy cadet, I attended a semester-long exchange at the French Air Force Academy in Salon-de-Provence in southern France. I had studied French for nearly ten years, but I'd never been to France before. I thoroughly enjoyed the experience from start to finish.

Back then, Princess Grace of Monaco was still alive. She grew up in Philadelphia as Grace Kelly and became a movie star before eventually marrying Prince Rainier. With an American heritage herself, she generously hosted a reception at the palace each autumn for the American cadets and their French sponsors. I didn't quite know what to expect. When we presented ourselves at the palace in our sharpest "Class A" uniforms, I was extremely nervous. Immaculately attired attendants ushered us into the ornate reception hall where we met Princess Grace. What then transpired convinced me that she had to be the most aptly named person ever.

As we presented the official protocol gift on behalf of the US Air Force, I was very relieved to feel Princess Grace's sincere warmth and respect for us. It shone through in every aspect of her demeanor and presence. She made us all feel very comfortable. I perceived that Princess Grace felt there was absolutely no other place in the world she wanted to be at that moment. Authentic or practiced? I firmly believe it was a genuine aspect of her character, developed and refined to a fine art through her graciously led life.

The almost surreal experience continued through the evening as I joined with another cadet to visit with Princess Grace's daughter, Princess Caroline, who was close to our age. Then, midway through our conversation, I heard the deep and distinct voice of Princess Grace's good friend Cary Grant as he chatted with yet another cadet. Cary was in town, so he had just dropped by for the evening!

This whole evening was completely foreign to my middle-class background as the son of a military man, and Princess Grace's genuine respect for and interest in us cadets made the night especially memorable. The princess, then one of the world's most famous people, had a beauty that extended deep into her gracious character. As an aside, I'm not certain that my grandmother, even after seeing the photographs, was ever totally convinced that her grandson had actually met Princess Grace.

I vowed that should I ever be in a position of high authority or become well known, I would respect the inherent dignity of anyone with whom I interacted, regardless of his or her position or rank. While I'm not particularly famous, astronaut life has given me some degree of unique public presence, and Princess Grace's superb example of grace that magical night decades ago has inspired my interactions with the many people I've met over the years. Recognizing their inherent worth as human beings and following that with a sincere interest in them has led to thousands of rewarding and, in many cases, touching human interactions.

Recognition and Strengthening: The Space Shuttle Seamstress

The day started at "zero-dark-thirty" with a two-hour T-38 flight from Houston to Kennedy Space Center. Once there, it dragged on interminably through a series of payload tests I was tasked to support. Finally, very late in the afternoon, the tests ended. Time to scoot out to the Shuttle Landing Facility (SLF), grab my (OK, "your," if you are a US taxpayer) T-38, and beat feet back to Houston.

For some reason, as I drove past the monstrous white-and-black Vehicle Assembly Building (VAB), I felt compelled to pop in to visit a few of the workers. By then, second shift, with its smaller staff, was well underway. Nearly all the shop windows were dark. When I peered through the door window into one of the few illuminated shops, I noticed a room full of sewing machines. The machines were large and industrial strength for sure, but they were sewing machines nonetheless. What could the maintenance team possibly do for the space shuttle in this shop?

When I called out hello, a quiet voice answered, "I'm here; come on back." I met a wonderful lady who seemed very close to retirement age. Of course, my first question was, "Why on earth do we have sewing machines in the VAB?" She replied, "Well, that's how we repair and refurbish the shuttle's thermal blankets." While the hottest surfaces required exotic tiles or brittle, reinforced carbon-carbon structures, the relatively cool topside could get by with lightweight soft goods. I knew about the blankets, but had never given any thought to their maintenance.

I had just met my first space shuttle seamstress! We had a wonderful conversation that started out with a few technical explanations. She showed me how she and her coworkers serviced the blankets. I explained that watching two thousand-degree, pinkish-orange plasma flowing by your window on reentry makes you very grateful you're nestled inside all of that amazing thermal protection. Thanking her for her dedicated service, I offered her my sincere recognition that her work was important, even crucial. As the conversation turned more personal, she showed me snapshots of her grandkids. I shared photos of my daughters, along with a heartfelt comment, "They appreciate what you do too!" The time flew by.

When we finally wound down our talk, she said something that placed this experience with a handful of the most gratifying personal interactions I ever had as an astronaut. As I took my leave, she said, "You know, I've worked out here over thirty years, and I've never met an astronaut before. Thank you so much for taking the time to come by." Her deep appreciation really touched me. Did my visit strengthen her? Because of what I represented, sure. However, I too was strengthened and encouraged in a deep, intangible way. The result: two members of America's space shuttle team were buoyed up for our future day-to-day service in an endeavor much bigger than ourselves.

You may not have the door-opening advantage of the astronaut flight suit as you make your rounds. Nevertheless, you and everyone on your team can still harness the power of mutual recognition and strengthening. If you are a leader, whether designated or not, take the time and make the effort for frequent, informal visits out where the work gets done. All it takes is a little bit of sensitivity and effort. The emails and action items will always be there, but the opportunities for the personal magic moments of human interaction may not.

Forging Links: Promoting Relationships

The very act of building the nodes of individual team members also contributes to forging the links between members. Furthermore, team members should take care to communicate directly, openly, and transparently with one another to build the right types of relationships. All should avoid the temptation to "triangulate" communications. Such triangulations are much like the old telephone game where you start a saying at one end of a line of people and repeat it across the group, ideally word for word. In reality, after surprisingly few repetitions, it is never anywhere close to verbatim.

Even with the best of intentions, indirect communications can lead to inaccuracies, rumor generation, and potentially hard feelings. Assuming everyone on the team is of goodwill, it still produces problems. If you have less forthright members intentionally working their own destructive ways for hidden personal agendas, it can be devastating to group unity.

I had an interesting, though at the time irritating, orbital situation that ties into such destructive agendas. Once a day in orbit, for just a few minutes, NASA Public Relations would allow a press interview with one of the crew. These events were usually pretty friendly affairs. As commander, I was looking forward to one last chance late in the mission to share the Neurolab story and the great work my crew had risked our lives to do. The originally scheduled radio network had needed to cancel. With very short notice, and apparently no vetting, NASA allowed a German print publication to interview me.

This newspaper was one of those types of rags marked by wanton disregard for the truth, the kind you see stocked by the grocery store checkout stand. After a few opening pleasantries, the interview quickly took an aggravating turn as the interviewer plunged into his own agenda, namely, that under no circumstances should we conduct any type of animal research. He declared that we were doing something horrible. I wanted to reach through the mic and across the ether to throttle the guy, but I simply responded with the truth: because NASA is a government agency, we very carefully follow every single ethical and legal requirement for the care and use of animals.

I wrapped it up as quickly as I could, still seething. The poor NASA public affairs person had to feel just awful, mortified even. I had a pointed little debriefing item, but I realized it could wait until my feet touched Earth. There was no urgent requirement that I reveal my irritation or call someone on the carpet in real time. I chose to tread gingerly in how I closed out the event, simply saying to our Mission Control (MCC) communicator (CAPCOM), Canadian astronaut Chris Hadfield, "Chris, of all the interviews I've ever given (very long, pregnant pause), that was one of them!" With a knowing tone, Chris replied, "Roger, Rick, we're bringing those comm loops down now." Regardless of the annoying interviewer, as an astronaut commander, I had to take a higher road. I also had a member of our bigger team, our public affairs specialist in the MCC, to consider. I saw no value in publicly humiliating her.

Recently, I've gotten a kick out of comparing my last public interaction from orbit with one our CAPCOM Chris Hadfield had much later in his career. In 2013, Chris commanded an International Space Station (ISS) expedition. As an accomplished guitarist and singer, he recorded his in-space performance of David Bowie's "Space Oddity." With Bowie's permission, it was released on YouTube and went viral, with over seven million views in short order. My space oddity was dealing with a screwy German interviewer; Chris Hadfield's was to turn into a rock star! Well deserved, though. He's a great guy and the best at sharing the magic of human spaceflight with folks down here on Earth.

Another aspect of forging links, a very positive one, also applies. Links are strengthened during common action. Joint effort and achievement produce a virtuous cycle. Through common action, relationships strengthen and team members desire to accomplish still more together. Although the scenarios may sometimes be artificial, there can be value in the myriad teambuilding exercises and activities you can employ. How much more value is generated when people work closely and directly together toward the actual business objectives of the team? Execution accomplishment feeds back to team development, which in turn spurs even crisper future execution.

Virtual teams can act effectively too. Today's superb information technologies leverage our team efforts magnificently. However, leaders guiding the most fully effective teams will always insist on a significant level of direct, face-to-face interaction and working together. Particularly early on in a team's life cycle, the personal touch pays high dividends.

It's really not even too much of a stretch to set as the first team activity a purely social get-together. It's an investment in forging the strong links that the team will need as the work gets more involved and difficult. The very first weekend after our crew assignment for STS-90, I set up a party for crewmembers and families so we could all start getting to know one another. As we began the journey that would ultimately lead to the crew risking our lives together, it was an important, high-return activity.

The ultimate forging value of doing things together comes when common action is directed toward purposeful objectives, the team overcomes significant obstacles, and an element of risk is involved and conquered. Perhaps it's partly adrenaline, but when my teams have acted in concert during physically risky operations and emergencies, we have bonded more effectively. Life-or-death teamwork really does take the team to a whole new level. You might not necessarily have the physical risks, but concentrate on having everyone pull together in the face of business uncertainties and other risks you do face.

Pouring the Cohesion Glue: Unity

Taking care of people along with building strong links and communications frames up a team matrix well. The last thing is to add the glue that holds it all together. Then you have that tough, resilient team, much like the robust composite materials modern engineering produces.

Many ingredients go into that glue. Organizationally, these factors can be subtle and intangible. Leaders need to find a way for everyone to contribute. Individual accomplishments should be encouraged, yet not at the expense of team achievements. Everyone needs to strive for deeper understanding of others' roles and skills. Even while bolstering their own specialized skill sets, team members need also to prepare sufficiently to shore up one another in tangible ways. Any act of backing up your teammate with time, work, or support builds unity. Mutual support translates to magnified results.

All must be sensitive to "too much of a good thing." For example, to build nodes, recognition is crucial. However, programs to recognize individuals must also align with promoting team values and goals. While competition within a team can be valuable, it needs to be bounded and held in check to some degree. There's no more competitive group of people in the world than a bunch of fighter pilots. There's also no group more team oriented when strapping on the jets to face a common foe, recognizing when internal competition needs to be subordinate to overall team unity.

No structure or program within an organization should allow one person to look good at the expense of others. Have you ever run across people who, through insecurity or lack of ability, live by the motto, "If you can't make yourself look good, then make someone else look bad"? Ouch, but those vipers are the worst sort of team killers! If allowed to work their ill will, team execution effectiveness plummets. Leaders, purge them at every opportunity. Others, do your best to work around such toxicity, recognize that eventually what goes around comes around, and not fall into the same trap.

Self-promoting, agenda-driven conflict within the team is obviously bad news. But the sincere, frank exchange of conflicting ideas, when all see how that process can eventually provide better results, will add to team cohesion. As long as everyone understands that it is with the team's benefit in mind, conflict too can be a cohesion glue.

Over the life of a given team, there will be thousands of interactions, some quite nuanced. Every exchange serves either to pour a little more glue into the matrix or introduce a unity-dispersing solvent. Working the Matrix properly requires a thoughtful and continual glue-pouring: the promotion of individuals, relationships, and every factor that would enhance the whole.

A Matrix to the Nth Power

No team can or should be entirely self-contained. External to the immediate team are peer groups, staff, stakeholders, bosses, customers, regulatory personnel, and competitors. The sheer size and complexity of today's large organizations, or complex projects like half billion dollar human space missions, dictate many sets of nested teams.

I learned to appreciate the multidisciplinary, sometimes convoluted, aspect of science research space missions while training for my first spaceflight. During that experience, I met many hundreds of great people in different NASA mission planning and operations teams, as well as principal investigator scientists from around the world. I saw firsthand how each team played a valuable part.

When I was assigned to command another complex research mission, the Work the Matrix concept had, in my mind, already expanded to "work the matrix to the nth power." The nth power view provides an opportunity and responsibility to look outside the immediate team and apply the same foundational principles with the "n" number of groups with which your immediate team interacts.

The first official duty I exercised as STS-90 Neurolab commander came the day after NASA publicly announced the full crew. It required my presence at NASA Headquarters in Washington, DC. I grabbed a T-38 from NASA Aircraft Ops and zipped up to Dulles International Airport. I always found it enjoyable to "zorch" into large commercial airports flying a sporty little T-38 Talon. Very fun to mix it up with all the heavy-iron airliners! Of course, as a military pilot astronaut, I was paid a lot less than those senior airline captains, but taxiing the little "rocket ship" by all those guys was its own reward.

I wasn't there for fun, though. The payload manager had given me some time to speak at a payload review conference of all the brilliant Neurolab life science principal investigators. These scientists were, in most cases, years into the team processes of preparing their experiments. However, this occasion would be the first time they would interact with the crew commander.

Now, I didn't really understand the complexities of their life-science research. I'm an engineer and pilot. I knew, however, that it was important to make a public commitment of support in front of this crowd. I looked the assembled scientists in the eye and assured them that I and every single member of the flight crew cared deeply about the experiments, recognized their value, and would work tirelessly to ensure success.

Soon it was time for Mr. CDR to back up his words with actions. I discovered that one particularly invasive experiment had also been ranked at the very top for the potential payoff and understanding it might deliver, so the scientists were keen on getting as much data as possible. Safety rules prevented me, as the commander, from participating in flight because the experimental setup was very constricting and could potentially hinder my response in case of an orbiter emergency. I learned, however, that the scientists would be ecstatic even to get just pre- and post-flight data from another crewmember, so I volunteered to let them play pin the tail on my vagus nerve before and after the flight. The only real cost to me was a little time for the data collection sessions and some minor discomfort. However, the broad, intangible team benefits far exceeded my hopes.

I was amazed at the positive feedback from the various nth power matrices during the year before the flight and then again post-flight. The fact that the operational "fly guy" had shown a high level of interest and then backed it up with actions seemed to surprise them. I also learned that through the previous twenty-four flight history of the Spacelab program, such commander enthusiasm was not universal. To me, it just seemed like the obvious, right thing to do. I understood that demonstrating deep support for the overall mission purpose paid significant relationship and team benefits.

Whether with your immediate team, other stakeholders, shareholders, or customers, Working the Matrix is a powerful tool. It will grow your people and unify your team. A cohesive team will pull together, exercising the unified action critical for proper execution.

—CUE CARD—

WORK THE MATRIX

CONSTANTLY CARE FOR
MATRIX OF INTERNAL AND EXTERNAL RELATIONSHIPS

Result: Working the Matrix leverages effective collaboration to get better results.

Team Benefit: Sincere care for individuals and relationships amplifies team unity.

Crew Notes for Business Execution:

8	"The matrix" is the set of all interrelationships within a team. Leaders must consider all the relationships and act to strengthen them.
7	Matrix nodes are individual team members. Building individuals up requires respect, recognition, strengthening, and training.
6	Respect recognizes the unique and important value of each person on the team, regardless of his or her role or experience level.
5	Recognition and strengthening should include formal programs and regular, informal acknowledgements of contributions.
4	Matrix links include all the formal and informal ways team members interact.
3	Links are strengthened via direct communications, face-to-face interactions, and conducting common actions, particularly when purposeful and including some element of risk.
2	Team cohesion requires strong nodes and links. Every single interaction within the team will either pour more cohesion glue or help dissolve it. Always work to enhance unity.
1	It's not just a matrix, but a matrix to the nth power, including all the external links with stakeholders, customers, and other teams. Everyone must be aware of all these outside relationships and carefully shepherd them.

Spaceflight Example: Effective team performance on a human spaceflight mission can be a matter of life or death. Building the necessary bonds for team cohesion in such extreme environments takes attention and diligent work in advance.

BUILD TOTAL TRUST

"The best way to find out if you can trust somebody is to trust them."
—Ernest Hemingway

Purposeful Performance Principle 9: More than any single factor, a high-trust culture enables capturing people's best efforts and contributions to meet the most challenging commitments.

U nquestionably, the most powerful unity-generating team factor is absolute trust. The higher the challenges before the team, the greater the need for that level of trust. A trust culture requires all team members, but particularly leaders, to consciously choose to be trustworthy. Trustworthiness consists not only of irreproachable integrity, but also of reliable competence. Choosing to be trustworthy implicitly demonstrates dedication to a larger purpose.

Poignant Goodbyes

It was Thursday, April 9, 1998, a week prior to the launch of STS-90. If a mission had no technical constraints, such as catching up to an orbital target for rendezvous, NASA would schedule space shuttle launches for a Thursday. With the increased countdown manning requirements starting three days prior to liftoff, Thursday resulted in having to pay the least amount of overtime. Go figure. Humorous, given all the other tremendously costly aspects of human spaceflight.

That evening, however, I wasn't particularly focused on amusing thoughts. It was time to enter quarantine, officially known as Astronaut Health Stabilization. Unlike Apollo, the Space Shuttle Program did not use dedicated backup crews. Quarantining the crew and limiting their activities mitigated the risks of a crewmember getting sick or injured close to launch.

The few adults allowed to see the crew, including spouses, needed to undergo a brief flight surgeon medical exam. They were also expected to refrain voluntarily from contact with the crew if feeling a cough or cold coming on. Children under the age of sixteen were not allowed in quarantine. As much as we love them, kids tend to pick up lots of germs at school and on the playground. So the docs correctly decreed, "No kids in quarantine."

I was in a serious, reflective mood, knowing that I wouldn't see my daughters for three weeks during this mission. Worst case, we wouldn't see one another again in this lifetime. Aged fifteen, twelve, and three, my girls were eagerly anticipating the adventure of heading down to Florida with other crew families, reconnecting with all the cousins and family friends, and visiting Disney World and the beach. Oh, and they would also get to see Dad blast off Pad 39B into space.

We had been through this goodbye drill twice before. These partings were the hardest part, emotionally, of the entire astronaut experience. The first time I left for space, the girls had little idea of the risks or dangers: "Bye, Daddy! Have fun! See you when you come back to Earth." For the second mission, the oldest two, Megan and Liz, were beginning to appreciate that Dad was going to do something risky. Prior to my third flight Megan had real concerns. By then, she knew all about the *Challenger* tragedy. There's clearly something different about the going-to-space goodbye compared to other farewells we've shared or the goodbyes most families have.

Daddy wasn't just headed out of town on a business trip. There was a real, albeit small, chance we'd never see one another again. That night, I left the house and my daughters and made the twenty-minute drive back to Johnson Space Center to enter into quarantine at Astronaut Crew Quarters. Like twice before, that drive seemed far longer than normal. I considered what my family would face if I couldn't return. It was, again, humbling, sobering, and emotionally draining.

Trusting Your Life to Your Team

Settling in with my crew once in quarters, however, the contemplative, concerned sentiments gave way to a warm, confident feeling. My dear friends— my brothers and sister—were unquestionably ready to go. I looked at them and said to myself, "Yep, I'm glad to trust my life to each of them." The five first-time space flyers and our other veteran, Rick Linnehan, had risen perfectly to every training and preparation challenge. All were principled, high-integrity people. I'd seen their quality of character over and over in the high-pressure crucible of crew training.

I also felt ready for my part as the crew commander. I recognized that other heartfelt leavings had taken place that evening. As commander, I had the most direct responsibility for crew safety and mission success. A few days later, all six of them were going to trust their lives to me as we sprung off the launch pad. Though confident, I also felt a deep obligation to my crew, their families, and all their friends.

No feeling in a team setting surpasses the confidence of having that level of trust in your colleagues. On three space missions and in my military and test flying world, I've many times been a member of teams where we absolutely trusted our lives to one another. In other settings through the years, though, I've also been in organizations that did not engage in such risky endeavors. In those teams as well, when my teammates and I knew we could trust our lives to each other if necessary, everything else fell marvelously into place.

First-Order Requirement: The Prime Directive

Like many astronauts, I'm a bit of a science fiction fan. In the *Star Trek* universe, the Prime Directive is the guiding principle that supersedes all else within the United Federation of Planets. It prohibits Starfleet personnel from interfering with any internal workings of alien civilizations, particularly those below a certain threshold of development.

This literary device set the conceptual stage for numerous great stories in all the *Star Trek* television shows and movies. It established a broad trust framework for the Federation. In recognition of the great power Starfleet Officers often held over others, the Prime Directive promoted trust. It was the single most important value and guiding light for all Starfleet actions.

Likewise, unimpeachable trust is the first-order requirement for team cohesion and success. It is, indeed, a prime directive itself. The trust-based team can work around the wide variety of human shortcomings, but gimmicks cannot compensate for a lack of trust. Absolutely nothing is more important for ultimate success in achieving team purpose. Many considerations, approaches, and philosophical underpinnings build that trust within a team. It rarely, if ever, comes entirely naturally. Correct leader attitude and example are necessary but not wholly sufficient. All team members must accept the criticality of the team reaching that trust level.

It takes directed effort to build a trust culture. Certain consciously applied techniques, coupled with an informal, genuinely right-minded way of being, synergistically build a high-trust culture. Make it your first-order team requirement, your prime directive. To do so, however, requires an even more fundamental prerequisite: every individual must firmly commit to being personally trustworthy.

Zeroth-Order Requirement: Trustworthiness

The zeroth-order requirement is the firm and irrevocable commitment on the part of every individual in the team to choose trustworthiness. As such, it is not an overall team quality per se, but instead an individual virtue vital to the team. Lack of trustworthiness in just one person on a team can wreak havoc. So what does being trustworthy really mean?

Worthiness implies deserving. Deserving comes from earning. Earning takes doing—doing what you say you'll do. We all must demonstrate to our peers, supervisors, and subordinates that we deserve the privilege of their trust. Trusting is, after all, an act of opening up our vulnerabilities. Why should others go out on a limb to count on us if we won't come through?

The basics apply. Being reliable, responsible, solid, steady, sure, constant, steadfast, dependable, and more all matter. Each is a trustworthiness building block. Old-fashioned qualities? Sure. Valuable in today's crazy world? Absolutely! Arguably, the breakneck pace of business today makes it more challenging than ever to track all the commitments we make, let alone actually meet them. The extra effort to do so is worth it, though. Teams filled with trustworthy, follow-through individuals maintain a strong competitive advantage. Trustworthiness, doing what you say you'll do, when and how you say you'll do it, resides at the very core of effective execution.

With so many people today not stepping up to the trustworthiness challenge, those who do will continue to shine brightly as the best contributors. As a commander and team leader in many ventures, I've always looked first to the consistently reliable, self-controlling, diligent individuals. Every boss should do the same. Trustworthiness is a key to individual success. When many trustworthy people add a key to the team key ring, then all the doors to the benefits of trust open wide.

Do we really have to aspire to such a high standard? Unquestionably, yes, if we truly want to enjoy the benefits of a trust-filled team. Those who take seriously this zeroth-order trustworthiness requirement will always enjoy a high payoff.

But what if everyone doesn't get with the program?

No Bad Apples

I once heard it attributed to a senior astronaut who'd served on many selection boards that the most important requirement is not that we choose the absolute best candidates, but that we get the best we can while avoiding hiring any bad apples. The individual who really has no sincere interest in working within a team—the less than fully trustworthy person—deserves no place in the Astronaut Corps.

Eventually, I had the opportunity to represent the Astronaut Office on the US Air Force astronaut nominating board. I kept that advice in mind as I, along with a board of seasoned USAF officers from many career fields, reviewed the records of astronaut hopefuls during that biennial process. I think we did an admirable job. Every Air Force astronaut selected in that group served with honor and distinction.

A few years later, an astronaut not from an Air Force background made the national news, and not in a good way. It was a sad and puzzling incident, with violated trust on many levels. Quickly dismissed from the Astronaut Corps, the individual's parent military service also issued a less-than-honorable discharge, a shameful but deserved fall-from-grace. The wisdom of choosing the best you can while focusing on not hiring any bad apples came back to my mind.

Occasionally, your team may find itself with someone who won't get with the program and can't be found worthy of trust. The leader, with support from the real team players, has to find the courage to remove the toxic influence from the team environment. It's a huge challenge to identify the specifics, document them, and then find the way to invite the team life-killer to depart. No one can offer a magic solution to this vexing problem, but leaders must always address it head on. Failure to do so will distract the team and, at worst, totally defeat any efforts at purposefully pulling together in coherent execution.

The Commander Sets the Tone

Even though every member of a team needs to strive for trustworthiness, one single member, the leader, constantly remains under the trust microscope. The leader must set the right tone and atmosphere for trust to flourish. It goes without saying that all aspects of his or her comportment, attitude, and even casual comments must consistently align with the highest integrity.

What more can leaders do, beyond being high-integrity people themselves, to foster the climate of trust within their teams? They can exercise a variety of techniques that consistently build trust-engendering relationships. These approaches generally fall into two categories: modeling the way and exercising capable humility.

First, leaders must model the way. Modeling the way includes, but goes beyond, maintaining high personal integrity. It requires showing utmost dedication to the mission and the team as an organization. Leaders need to offer positive, uplifting communications to and about people internal or external to the team. You are constantly sending overt and subtle signals, all of which are subject to the team's interpretation. Make certain the signals clearly and unequivocally support right values and actions. It is a pull, not a push, planted squarely on the right path and beckoning others, through example, to follow.

Don't ever be one to "throw someone under the bus." Few actions are more destructive to what trust may have been developed. The team will close down. Though pathways of trust within the team may still exist, alliances will align with self-protection. Effort will focus on mutually defending against the offender—instead of completing the mission. Such a climate is pernicious, deadly to team trust, and prevents accomplishing productive, mission-oriented work.

It's said that perception is reality. Often it really isn't. However, when it comes to teams observing leaders, perception absolutely is reality. When the leader always aligns his or her behavior with what's right, from the big stuff down to the smallest detail, the team can tell. Then the sense of security grows. Everyone feels more comfortable and confident in "exposing their flanks." That comfort allows the needed interdependencies to develop. The trust expands.

Modeling the way through example sets the perfect tone. In itself it will go a long way in establishing the needed trust environment. Leaders also have the opportunity to take trust to an even higher level. The means comes through the combination concept I've termed "capable humility."

Exercising Capable Humility

The complementary second category of trust-building techniques requires the leader to practice capable humility. The leader, already modeling the way with the right example, can leverage that example tremendously through this approach. This practice also proves particularly effective for the informal leaders in a team—in other words, every single team member.

The ability to apply capable humility marks extraordinary team builders. It begins with the capable element. Effective leaders must be confident and adept. In fact, no matter how high the integrity, it's difficult to trust a leader who just isn't particularly competent. People's common sense protective shields prevent it.

Although nearly every military leader I served under was thoroughly competent and earned my confidence, one rare exception stands out. This relatively senior squadron officer was a decent, well-meaning person, but limited in capability. He certainly didn't fit as a leader in the dynamic, unforgiving world of a fighter squadron. When the junior pilots give you the nickname "Boo Boo," it doesn't indicate they trust your abilities! Of course, the nickname remained a secret from him. Occasionally it was funny to watch him flail in the squadron, but it was never funny in the air.

One dark, moonless night over the North Sea, Boo Boo could not complete a successful hookup with an air refueling tanker. He then compounded the competence shortfall with the poor judgment to keep trying as he went well below "bingo" fuel, the amount needed to get back over land to any available runway. Fortunately, he managed to connect and take on some fuel eventually. His incompetence violated the trust of the young WSO in his right seat, who was rightfully very concerned about a night ejection over frigid winter waters. Somewhat shaken after the experience, he came back into the squadron that night vowing never to fly with Boo Boo again.

Assuming that you, as a leader, know your stuff and have the requisite capability, what's next? The exercise of that competence in humility amplifies the positive effect. Such individuals are willing to give people a job and let them do it without micromanaging. Jack Welch, noted former CEO of General Electric, often exclaimed that he loved to hire people smarter than himself. Humbly acknowledging others' strengths is the key first step to effective delegation, a form of capable humility. Delegation is at its core a placing of trust.

Capably humble leaders listen proactively and carefully. They don't hide behind email or other impersonal forms of communication, especially on the tough issues. These leaders want the feedback, whether it's good or provides an opportunity for improvement. They get out of the office and seek it out, making the face-to-face connections. The more that happens, the more team members are willing to open up. Trusting pathways grow.

Fostering consensus expands the trusting communications pathways further. Perhaps almost counterintuitively, promoting frank, open discussions is what will lead to eventual consensus. Team members need to feel comfortable hashing out conflicting, strongly held opinions in the process. Everyone needs to trust that voicing those alternate viewpoints openly won't come back to threaten them. Conflict can be very productive when couched in full, trusting knowledge that everyone's pulling for the team first. With capable humility, the leader encourages all ideas and positions, validating a trust-based communications and solutions development methodology.

Finally, capable humility requires a balanced recognition that we all make mistakes. It reinforces team trust for members to recognize that for honest mistakes, second chances will be the norm. Furthermore, the transparent leader, who openly admits his or her own mistakes along with an action plan to move forward, truly lives capable humility. Such transparency and trust will only continue to strengthen the team.

The Check-Six Mindset

As the leader sets the tone and has many tools available to promote trust, the right collective mindset continues to build upon the leader-established foundation. One of the key cultural attributes of trusting teams is a mutual support attitude known as "Check-Six."

Check-Six is a well-known term used in military aviation. Physically, it speaks to the absolute necessity to scan constantly for threats, particularly right behind you (the six o'clock position). Since it is at best difficult to look directly behind you and, depending on aircraft design, maybe impossible, you must always rely on other pilots in your formation to check your six. Your wingman or flight lead and other fellow team members need to back you up to protect you.

As an attack pilot in F-111s, without a good rear field of view (as with a bubble canopy in newer tactical aircraft), relying on your wingman to check your six was a life-or-death imperative to defend against air and ground threats. Although in its day the Vark could outrun anything flying at low altitude if you could see it in time, death would come from what you could not see. The ability to dash to nearly a thousand miles per hour at sea level wouldn't help you if you never saw a threat and so missed the chance to accelerate out from a relatively pedestrian six hundred miles per hour!

More abstractly, the Check-Six attitude infuses every activity within a military flying squadron. These organizations are invariably full of competitive, high-achieving individuals. With a team-oriented mutual support culture, nearly all of them are concurrently bastions of the highest levels of trust.

The concept is so powerful that a consulting firm named Check Six has found tremendous success transferring these lessons to the oil exploration industry, particularly offshore oil rig operations. I had the privilege early in the company's history to work with its former US Navy fighter pilot founders in developing the concept. Now the amazing company they've built has a presence on the majority of the offshore rigs worldwide, reinforcing high-trust teams in dynamic and dangerous environments.

Your team operations environment may not be as challenging as the flight deck of an aircraft carrier or the drilling platform of an offshore oil rig. Nevertheless, you still need trustworthy individuals all checking six to magnify team trust levels for sterling execution in your own fast-paced settings.

Dream Crews

Two years into my astronaut tenure, I had learned a lot. I'd also begun to contribute directly as a "Cape Crusader," a member of the astronaut support team for the real spacecraft and hardware at KSC. I enjoyed every duty I had in that hands-on, operational job. To my knowledge, though, a mission assignment was still a ways away.

As I walked down the hall one day, experienced astronaut Shannon Lucid stepped out of her office. "Hi, Rick. How are things going down at the Cape?"

"Great, Shannon, very busy."

"Rick, do you know what the most important thing about a crew assignment is?"

"Oh, that maybe I'll eventually get one?"

"Well, sure, of course. Beyond that, though, it's not about being assigned to the most glamorous or exciting mission. What you really want is to be assigned to a crew where everyone gets along, where you totally trust one another."

Food for thought. "By the time launch comes, you'll have spent so much time together you'll all either love one another or be sick of each other. I've been on both types of crews, and the first, no matter what the mission itself entails, is by far the best."

"Thanks, Shannon. I can definitely see all that."

A week later, Chief Astronaut Dan Brandenstein called me into his office. "Rick, we have a mission assignment for you. You'll pilot STS-58 on *Columbia*." Ecstatically, but professionally, I responded, "Thank you! I really appreciate the opportunity." Internally, it was, *Woo-hoo! Oh yeah, I'm going to space!*

Shannon must've known in advance of the impending crew assignment and that she and I were to be crewmates; she always knew everything happening in the Astronaut Office. She was also absolutely right. I can't imagine a better group with whom to fly in space than the STS-58 crew. It was indeed a dream crew: a superb people experience from start to finish.

I've been privileged to work with many trust-based teams through the years besides the STS-58 crew. I hope you experience your own high-trust teams. Work to develop that trust. Your mission will flow better. The time will pass more enjoyably. Your team will execute more crisply and the accomplishments will be greater and more gratifying.

Trust Your Ground Team

Mid-mission during STS-90, I was on the flight deck performing CDR duties when Kay Hire floated up and said, "Rick, I just heard an odd whirr and clunk coming from under the middeck floor. Sounds like something's wrong with the RCRS [Regenerative Carbon Dioxide Removal System]." The RCRS was an important life support system that scrubbed excess carbon dioxide from our air. It was a newly developed system intended to increase shuttle mission duration; STS-90 was one of its first flights.

After Kay's heads-up, I accessed the RCRS data on *Columbia's* computer screen to discover a malfunction signature unlike any I'd ever seen in training. Houston quickly informed me that it was a new failure mode to them as well. They instructed us to use the backup system while they worked the problem. Our mission planning team had made the risk-mitigating decision to also load a few days' worth of carbon dioxide absorbing lithium hydroxide canisters for backup. We did not have stowage space for all the bulky canisters required to support a full mission, but having enough loaded to carry us through any RCRS troubleshooting period was, as it turned out, a very wise move. We were in a safe configuration for the time being, but full mission success required resolving the problem.

My concern as CDR was that, if we couldn't fix the device, we would have to cut short our mission by about a third, losing a tremendous amount of scientific return. Once I turned the challenge over to our amazing colleagues in Houston, however, I had the utmost confidence that they would expeditiously solve the problem, even though it had never been seen before. That confidence rested in a deep trust borne of experience that MCC had the technical talent, organizational setup, and culture to quickly find a solution. As I returned to my other duties, I left them to work their magic, barely even thinking about the RCRS for the next two days.

While we continued our normal orbital activities, the flight director put together a classic NASA "tiger team" to come up with a fix. After two solid days and nights of troubleshooting with the RCRS ground test article, the team understood our failure and came up with a fix. We learned later that the team leader had been a junior life support engineer on the Apollo 13 "failure is not an option" team that saved Jim Lovell's crew. We definitely had the varsity on duty.

MCC sent us a procedure where Scott and I pulled several middeck lockers out of the way, accessed the system, and fixed it by rerouting some air lines. It happened to be a Saturday down in Houston, so I quipped after thanking the tiger team for their superb work, "If I were home, I'd probably be working on my car anyway." With an effective response built upon correct technical and organizational principles, the ground team had superbly validated our trust in them. While our situation wasn't nearly as critical as Apollo 13's, preserving a half-billion dollar mission is still nontrivial. The success came thanks to a culture developed through years of dealing with the unknown in many human space missions.

As leaders, we need to build the trust culture within our nth power matrices as well as the immediate team. External trust-building interactions and support are important for us to create the necessary levels of trust with our own "ground teams." With a broad trust culture, you can then rely on their support when you need it to preserve your mission.

—CUE CARD—

BUILD TOTAL TRUST

ESTABLISH, MODEL, LIVE
HIGHEST TRUST CULTURE

Result: A trust culture enables capturing the best contributions to meet difficult commitments.

Team Benefit: Absolute trust founded on leader trustworthiness is the single most important factor for team unity and ultimate performance.

Crew Notes for Business Execution:

9	The more difficult the tasks, the more compelling the need for the highest trust culture.
8	Absolute trust generates greater team confidence than any other quality or activity.
7	The first-order requirement for leaders is to direct conscious effort toward modeling and building the highest trust within the team.
6	Meeting the first-order requirement for a trust culture requires the zeroth-order individual commitment from each team member to be trustworthy.
5	Mistakes are forgivable, but willfully violating trust is not. You must find a way to purge those who violate trust.
4	While all team members need to be trustworthy, the commander sets the tone and so must hold to the very strictest standards while constantly communicating the highest valuation of integrity and competence.
3	Capable humility amplifies the trust-building effect of integrity. It requires adept competence, careful listening, fostering consensus, and forgiveness of honest mistakes.
2	A Check-Six mutual support and backup mentality is a key cultural attribute of high-trust, effectively executing teams.
1	The dream crew is not the one doing the most glamorous work, but the one whose members could trust their lives to one another.

Spaceflight Example: Astronauts literally trust their lives to one another, over and over, in every flight phase.

PART III
PERSPECTIVE: THE HOW

Perspective is the repository of the collective "big picture." We need to convert the fancy words of vision and mission statements, plans, and goal and objective lists into internalized ways of thinking and being. Perspective helps us make that conversion. The teams that don't follow through on the initial elements of purpose typically lack the wisdom of perspective. Conversely, people who work hard to maintain the right perspective more effectively focus on their purpose. Strong, appropriate values drive wise perspective. Wisely seeking balance in thoughts, culture, and action also reinforces perspective. Cultivating perspective pulls everything else together in gearing up to execute exquisitely.

While the profound experience of seeing planet Earth from space gives one an entirely new perspective on most everything, anyone can cultivate the variety of outlooks informing a 4P Perspective. This book presents two vital dimensions of perspective, both actionable and relevant. When it comes to purpose-powered execution excellence, maintaining balance in thought and action and keeping operations in line with values-driven principles are powerful keys.

With balance, team members can maintain for the long run, bounce back, and endure to complete the job—all essential execution requirements. Humor, breaks, reenergizing the team, fitness, resilience, and realistic optimism contribute too. Balance is reflected daily in outlook and attitudes that invariably will feed into tangible results.

A values-driven, principled approach is another long-term key to success. It promotes clear and stringent performance and behavior standards. Principled norms empower quality individuals and winnow out those of lesser mettle and integrity. First-principle orientation serves as one of the most powerful focusing tools for actions aligned with objectives.

BALANCE THE ORBIT

"Some people see the glass half full. Others see it half empty. I see a glass that's twice as big as it needs to be."

—George Carlin

Purposeful Performance Principle 8: A positive yet reality-grounded perspective sets the stage for highest team member engagement, productivity, and results.

P erspective requires balance. Leaders with balanced perspectives set the right tone through modeling the correct mix of humor, resiliency, and stress relief. Fitness, a confident but not too serious self-concept, and realistic optimism all contribute to balanced team effectiveness. That balance, in turn, promotes the necessary remembrance of purpose.

Connected to a Billion

"So, Dave, we're looking at nearly a billion people right now." My Canadian crewmate, Dr. Dave Williams, floated next to me near *Columbia*'s overhead flight deck windows. The day's payload work was completed, our delicious freeze-dried dinners were digesting, and our short, daily medical conference with the flight surgeons in Mission Control was all wrapped up. We had a few precious minutes to drink in the spectacular views from 170 miles up.

Behind lay eastern China. The sweeping panorama included the extensive gray smudge marking Beijing nestled up against the Luliang Mountains. Right below swirled the muted colors of the Yellow Sea's coastal waters. The corrugated mountain landscape of the Korean Peninsula pointed toward us from the north, and to the south stretched the east China coast, Shanghai, and the Yangtze River delta. At the far southern horizon, we could barely see the northern tip of Taiwan. There really were close to a billion people in our field of view.

Dave's reflective reply: "I can't help but feel connected to them, even though we're so separated." I felt the same. From an orbital perch, you can see how we are all in it together on this cosmic journey. We were orbiting the sun with the other six billion people on the planet even while our spaceship, *Columbia,* whirled around Spaceship Earth. The entire solar system was in turn hurtling through our galaxy at prodigious speed. "What a gift, isn't it, to have the chance to be up here and have this view, to see Earth from this perspective?" I said. We continued our discussion as *Columbia* and her seven humans coasted out over the vastness of the Pacific and approached the night side of the planet. Then we quietly, almost reverently, soaked up a sublime orbital sunset.

Beholding planet Earth from space is a deeply moving experience. It's a gift I wish could be given to everyone in the human family. As we viewed this overwhelming panorama from our unique vantage point, I felt very small, yet confident that I and my fellow humans were of great worth and importance. I returned with an enhanced yearning to truly understand what my, and our, place in the universe really is. It was extremely uplifting emotionally and imbued me with a renewed sense of grand-scale optimism for the human family.

When I returned from my first spaceflight, I vowed always to remember and treasure the feelings stirred by seeing the Earth from orbit. More crucially,

I determined I would act on them to try to serve as a positive, uplifting influencer for good. It would have been even better had the experience been so life-changing that it not only inspired me, but also erased some of my own human foibles. When I returned to the home planet, alas, my own impatient nature and personal weaknesses still remained. For example, I still occasionally yelled at my kids or screamed in frustration at the Houston traffic. Nevertheless, seeing the Earth from those perspectives and enjoying the great privilege of spaceflight did evolve my viewpoint. Experiences such as this one looking back at China made me consider more carefully many of the more intangible elements of life, relationships, and what's truly important. It drove home the value of seeking the "big picture" perspective and laboring to gain a measure of wisdom. The overall lesson for me was to strive for balance in all these things.

The balance of intangibles that makes certain teams truly successful is often hard to identify or replicate. That "special sauce" supplements, but certainly doesn't replace, organizing and executing on core principles. It certainly can make the crucial difference between the very best and the also-rans.

Attitudes and team dynamics that enhance a team's balanced perspective are very powerful in generating potent team chemistry. A grounded, healthy team outlook on the venture promotes clear thinking and wise decisions. Balance in effort and attitude within the team optimizes performance and keeps it focused on the most important aspects. With so many ways to introduce and reinforce balanced perspective in team environments, it could be the subject of an entire book itself. For our purposes here, we'll focus on key aspects universally applicable to either earthbound or spacefaring teams.

Keep It Light, Even While Dealing with the Serious

I believe it's fair to say that certain requirements of an astronaut's work make it one of the highest pressure jobs possible. Performance matters, and the whole world's watching—or at least it will be if you mess up! Execute or die, to put it bluntly. When in the crunch with an emergency or critical phase, you'd better get it right. So you work and train very, very hard to make sure you're up for the task.

The same goes for whatever line of work you're in. Hunker down and take your job seriously. Nevertheless, a serious, even stressful job does not mean you shouldn't cultivate a sense of humor in the workplace. Through the years, the teams I most enjoyed were the ones where everyone felt comfortable with the occasional quip or even practical joke. Not coincidentally, such groups also tend to execute more effectively than more uptight organizations. To break the ice, it helps to provide interim breaks during a pressure-packed meeting—really it helps to do so any time when the breaks are not a distraction to getting the job done—and teams can always benefit from and enjoy a little wit along the way. Even if he or she is not a stand-up comedian, the wise leader who shows a sense of humor will build a tighter team.

Following my second spaceflight, I served as a branch chief in the Astronaut Corps. My duties included attending a Monday morning meeting and status report session with the Chief Astronaut and the half-dozen other branch chiefs. We were essentially the Astronaut Office leadership council, dealing with significant and important operational issues constantly. The Chief Astronaut at the time, a US Marine Corps Colonel named Bob Cabana, could be as intensely serious as you would imagine any Marine might be. However, Bob's keen sense of humor and appreciation for the occasional lighthearted comment led to great dynamics within his teams.

One Monday morning, Bob walked into the meeting and announced, "Guys, you're not going to believe this, but we just hired a set of identical twins for the next astronaut class." Everyone sat quietly for a few seconds until I asked him, "But, boss, how do you know you actually interviewed both of them?"

With all of us knowing just how intense the astronaut selection process is, my offhand comment must've struck a funny chord—everyone burst out laughing.

Chuckling, Bob replied, "Well, we think we did."

By the way, those two twins, Mark and Scott Kelly, went on to superb careers in the Astronaut Corps. Mark commanded *Endeavour's* last flight. In addition to commanding a space shuttle mission, Scott has served one previous long-duration tour aboard the International Space Station and launched again in March 2015 for the first-ever year-long stay aboard ISS.

Building in Pressure-Relief Valves

The higher the stress your team is under, the more it needs to have just the right safety valves in place to deal with the pressure-packed environment. I found this principle incredibly useful in high-stress team settings. Having previously experienced the high pressure on a mission with very challenging objectives and knowing that the extremely ambitious Neurolab schedule would generate much the same type of stress, we decided to build in a few safety valves.

The first was simple: eat dinner together as a crew. What? You might think that seven people all cooped up in a tin can must be constantly bumping into one another all day, every day. You see plenty of one another, right? Not necessarily. You could pass an entire day when, because of divergent work activities, you just occasionally zoomed past other crewmates, barely interacting.

Everyone on the crew breaking bread together, or maybe bouncing M & M's off the walls together in weightlessness, gave a chance to review the day's work, discuss the next day's activities, decompress, and even listen to some music together. One of our teammates, Dr. Jay Buckey, put together a set of crew songs for the dinner hour. His song list was a mix of our actual favorites and some other rather ridiculous ones for the sake of good humor. Imagine floating around in weightlessness listening to Wayne Newton's "Danke Schoen." Get the picture? These crew dinners, bonding experiences all, not only provided some of the best memories of the mission, but also helped us mentally prepare for the next day's work.

On day ten, the crew's evening meal gave us the chance to play a major food joke on a teammate. The target was Scott "Scooter" Altman, who grew up in Illinois farm country and, at six foot four inches and roughly 225 pounds, was the world's biggest astronaut. During our preflight session at the food lab as we tested menu items, the rest of us discovered that, big as he was, Scott was a bit of a picky eater. During that sampling lunch, about every third food item received the response, "No, I don't like this one."

Midway through the evolution, I started taking notes, not for serious reasons, but for orbital pressure-relief purposes. Later, I coordinated with the NASA dieticians to have them replace Scott's color-coded menu items for the evening meal on flight-day ten with all the stuff he most disliked. Of course I did not care to have the world's biggest astronaut ticked off at dinner time in the middeck, so I also had them provide his selected items for my menu that evening.

Everyone was in the know except Scooter. Out came his yellow-dot-marked dinner entrée: eggplant parmesan. "Hey, I ordered steak for tonight!" Then some less-than-desirable vegetable side dish. "I hate this stuff. What gives?" Finally, the coup de grâce: tapioca pudding. "Yuck, those food lab folks are going to hear about this in the debriefing!"

"Hey, Scooter," I said.

"Yes, boss?"

Then all six of his crewmates, laughing in unison, exclaimed, "Gotcha!"

"Scott, you can have my steak. In fact, let's just swap everything." I was fine with the eggplant. I'll eat pretty much anything.

You can and should find a place for humor in any team setting. It's a fantastic lubricant. It helps forge links and loosens up the team. Of course, jokes and humor need to be balanced and appropriate. Keep an eye out for the many opportunities to proactively create these types of interactions.

Don't Take Yourself Too Seriously: Reactive Version

Good-natured jokes and lighthearted humor initiated within the team are all well and good. However, another aspect to not taking yourself too seriously is equally important for healthy team dynamics. I call this aspect the reactive version, as in our reactions to the negative. How ready are you or your teammates to take umbrage? Do you take slights personally, or are you able to brush them off? Dealing with misunderstandings can be trying within the best of teams, depending upon many constantly evolving factors. It does not help if one or more team members have personal "trip wires" set up.

Your team members should not have to tiptoe around one another. Cultivate the "water off a duck's back" approach. The ability to do this is primarily based on trust. Leaders should encourage attitudes that allow people the confidence to think well of themselves, but not get puffed up. That combination will build the "wise space" between a negative stimulus and an overreaction.

If allowed, anyone can find multiple irritations every day to take personally in a negative way. Conversely, the more good humor leaders and other team exemplars inject into the environment, the more confidently and positively the entire team will react. One of the most effective leaders with whom I ever served constantly reminded us that, no matter what the task or challenge, we "Madhatters" of the 492nd Tactical Fighter Squadron should go after it with unflinching "enthusiasm and good humor." I've never forgotten this saying as I saw how powerful his continual reinforcement was in leading us to superb operational success.

It can be a temptation for anyone, but particularly a highly successful, hard-charging professional, to react personally more than he should. It could even potentially happen the day after you bring Uncle Sam's two billion dollar spaceship home safe and sound. Arriving back in Houston after our KSC landing of *Columbia*, our STS-90 crew enjoyed with our families a nice little welcome home ceremony at Ellington Field, near JSC. The main purpose for these events was to give returning crews the chance to thank our mission support teams and meet any of the general public who cared to come out. As it all wrapped up, we were the last ones there, well after normal business hours.

NASA was supposed to have sent transport for us. We crew all had our cars parked miles away at the quarantine facility. Besides, the flight surgeons didn't want returning astronauts to drive for a few days after coming home from space due to balance deficits as we readapted to gravity. The problem arose when the transport vans never showed. We didn't have cell phones. Yep, stranded, with no way home. How soon they forget! After a journey of six and a half million miles, we came up just a few miles short of getting to our own homes. We had brought *Columbia* back in one piece, but now we were old news, totally forgotten and marooned!

I got a big kick out of watching the crew's response. Although no one was any longer a rookie space flyer, we still had five rookie "returning space flyers." It didn't help either that we were all still physically and mentally exhausted. We had a couple folks start to get a bit perturbed. The ironic humor of the situation did not quite appeal to them. I said to everyone, "Welcome back to Earth, guys! This is the way it really is. We're now officially yesterday's news!" We eventually discovered an open hangar door, reached a phone, and got in touch with the somewhat embarrassed transportation dispatcher.

Life's too short. There's no use dying all tensed up—especially when the tension's self-induced.

Bounce Right Back

You're human; get over it! Everyone on your team is human; get over that too. You will all make mistakes. You will suffer setbacks. But the great news about being human is that we humans are inherently adaptable. It's perhaps our greatest strength as a species, so don't ever discount it. A balanced and astute understanding of our basic resilient nature is crucial within the team.

What elements of a balanced organizational structure amplify that inherent resilience, instead of reducing it? First, incorporate as much diversity of thought, experiences, and background within your team as possible. Such a balanced array within the team provides necessary foundational structure to then craft various backup protections within the team. With the advantages of that breadth, the team is positioned to cover many more eventualities.

Today's complexity has a tendency to drive organizations to ever more specialization. While specialization may be necessary, it is definitely not sufficient. To reinforce systemic resilience within a team, you must prepare and train different team members to cover critical roles for one another. Modularize critical functions, or in other words, develop separate, parallel execution paths for the most important team activities. Mindfully introduce some overlap between team member roles where it makes sense.

For my STS-90 crew, we laid out at the start of training a huge chart showing every single anticipated crew activity for the flight. Then, in consultation with the crew, I assigned a primary, secondary, and, in most cases, a third person for each role. Many assignments were a natural consequence of our background and crew position. For example, I was to land *Columbia* with Scott as backup. Dr. Rick Linnehan, our veterinarian astronaut, was to take the lead on the orbital animal surgeries. A whole host of other activities, such as who would act as "suit technician" to get everyone else in their pressure suits before reentry, were not so straightforward and required a lot of thought, discussion, and tradeoffs.

We considered every possibility we could think of and systematically assigned and trained alternate crewmembers for each event. That overlap gave us much greater resilience for recovery from the inevitable schedule and equipment malfunction issues that could've prevented the work from getting done. The important consideration was to consciously address how our team would incorporate both depth and breadth to make us many-fault tolerant. You can and should do likewise.

Building as much predictability and controllability as possible into the team setting contributes to a bounce-back team. Of course, most of our environment, what our competitors do, the broader economy, and so forth are essentially out of our control and extremely difficult to predict. Accordingly, training and experience, drills, tabletop discussions, "what-if" sessions, and the like are absolutely necessary. These team activities, persistently undertaken, help reduce the number of unpleasant and unexpected surprises. Offering team members as much choice as possible in work definition and standards, timeframes, and accountability requirements also builds a more confidently adaptable culture.

Go into execution with a levelheaded view of what you may face. That balanced perspective will help you create the structure and culture to bounce back confidently from your own mistakes and the externally created messes that fall your way. Strive to bolster inherent team resilience with the ability to absorb your imperfections, shake off the mistakes, and get back to it.

Fit for the Work

For many people, the term "fitness" just brings up guilty feelings about not having kept their New Year's resolution to start working out. Even when considered more positively, it is often taken as a separate aspect of our lives, entirely independent from our work. At its core, however, fitness is the quality of being suitable to fulfill a particular role or task. It's indisputable that our fitness level can contribute markedly to our overall ability to work productively and energetically in our profession.

I've enjoyed being in professions where a certain level of physical fitness was an absolute must for selection and performance of the work. Ever since running track and playing soccer in high school, I've loved to exercise. I've found the benefits very helpful in all aspects of my job performance. Moreover, when working with like-minded individuals, it has definitely boosted overall team performance and readiness to execute.

Contrary to some popular stories or movies, you do not need to be some sort of super athlete to be an astronaut. No "radical vertical impact test," dropping you head first from heights like in the movie *Spies Like Us* is required! A better than average level of fitness, strength, and endurance is necessary, though. General fitness definitely allows you to keep up with the demands of training, flight, and recovery when you come back to Earth. Specific fitness for certain roles also matters. For example, grip strength is required for spacewalks; hand/eye coordination and fine motor skills must be refined to manually fly the orbiter with precision on landing; and extensive, on-orbit leg strength must be maintained to withstand gravity after six months on a space station. All these levy different fitness training requirements on crewmembers.

I also appreciate how a fitness deficit can hinder the ability to complete a goal. Over a period of several months during Air Force pilot training, I had a number of seemingly unrelated instances of severe abdominal cramps. Once, I even had to be hospitalized overnight. The severe episodes always subsided; fortunately, the debilitating, doubled-over cramping never came on while flying solo. I also felt very fatigued most of the time. I just attributed it to the long hours and very early 2:30 a.m. wakeups. It was just the way it was. That was fine until my appendix, which in retrospect we realized had been acting up for months, finally burst. After surgery and a longer hospital stay to heal from the peritonitis, I felt like a totally new man. Once back on the flying schedule, my performance skyrocketed, and I went from being a good T-38 student pilot to the top of my class in instruments and formation. Since then, thanks to that dramatic contrast, I've doubly appreciated my health and the ability to work.

How does fitness tie into balancing your orbit? In the sense that it is an element of work/life balance that can improve energy levels brought into the workplace, it's definitely of value. Where there is at least a cultural acknowledgement of the value of reasonable fitness and wellness levels, teams tend to have higher energy and enthusiasm. Recognizing that most business team settings do not have job-specific physical fitness performance standards, team leaders still should promote wellness and fitness concepts where possible.

Promoting fitness needs to be approached tactfully and with respect for individual choices. Still, enlightened leaders and teams acknowledge the organizational return in supporting team member fitness. Leaders also should sensitively engage with fellow team members to appreciate where health issues can induce some limitations so as to back one another up. With a balanced and holistic view that anything boosting the ability of team members to perform is an asset, everyone on the team should balance specific work activities with a choice also to maintain his or her own overall fitness levels.

Realistic Optimism

I'm not naturally optimistic. Perhaps few test pilots are. As a test pilot with an engineering background, I generally take a pretty practical, no-nonsense approach to endeavors. Actually, you don't really want your test pilot to take an aircraft through its paces and come back with nothing but happy, mushy words. It is not a "kumbayah" profession! You want and need to identify deficiencies so you can fix them.

The same serious approach to improvement in any team venture should apply. Unrealistic and unwarranted denial of reality for the sake of silver-lining-type optimism is not useful. At best, it temporarily pumps up the team. At worst, it can lead to skeptical or even cynical attitudes as capable individuals perceive widening gaps between reality and hype. Without accepting the real difficulties you face, traipsing through your challenges wearing rose-colored glasses can actually be self-defeating in the long term.

Regardless of how daunting your challenges seem, a well-grounded attitude that you can find the way to overcome them is a powerful and execution-oriented form of optimism. You must relentlessly ferret out the problems, then confidently gather the team to brainstorm all the many ways you can fix them. Consciously work hard to recognize that the difficulties need not be permanent or all-consuming.

When I flew the very first flight of the XCOR experimental rocket-powered X-Racer aircraft, we discovered an alarming issue. As we built up to our highest speed test point of the flight, the control surfaces started a disconcerting and potentially very dangerous buzz-type vibration. I immediately backed off, and we came home to some worried engineers. With concern for dropping behind in the program and initially no idea what was causing this unexpected flight safety issue, the team was quite taken aback. The mood was sober.

In the debriefing, it quickly became obvious to me that I needed not only to report the test pilot technical observations, but to offer some team encouragement as well. "Guys, something like this always happens on early test flights. Let's be grateful we had a conservative buildup plan for the flight that let us discover it early and safely. You'll run it to ground and fix it quite soon, I'm positive."

With renewed energy, the team more optimistically set about discovering and solving the problem. It ended up that the ailerons themselves, the control surfaces that allow the aircraft to roll left or right, were out of mass and balance specifications. It had been built and documented incorrectly prior to delivery to XCOR. We got it fixed quickly enough, along with an important lesson. Discovering the problem highlighted the criticality of every little thing in flight test and enhanced the confidence-building process of knowing we could find and solve the unknown problems that would arise.

Seek the Golden Linings

Realistic, execution-focused optimism is always wiser than an "everything will work out fine, but I don't have to do anything" hope. After all, hope is not a plan. If you consider the positive but passive view as silver-linings optimism, you must do better. Take it to the next level with a proactive and confident problem-solving viewpoint. I call that type of conscious and grounded confidence "golden-lining optimism."

During one orbit, overhead the Amazon River basin, a monstrous thunderstorm far below caught my eye. It happened to be sitting right underneath the terminator, that moving line between night and day on the planet, as nighttime approached the storm's location. Consequently, the side of the storm facing us was lit with an extremely low sun angle that created a cheery, rosy-golden glow on the lower reaches of the storm and highlighted every feature of the clouds. Scrambling for the camera, I managed to capture several photographs. Back on Earth, we discovered that the photos were among the most stunning thunderstorm images ever captured from space.

Those images became my proof-positive that not every cloud has a silver lining. It can be even better, with a golden lining! Metaphorically, it represents the buoyant attitude that, no matter what the challenge, our team is up to the task. Although we might have to work harder than ever before, we nonetheless have the willpower, talent, and desire to overcome. Regardless of one's own concerns or feelings of inadequacy, promoting such an attitude is a key execution leadership tool.

A balanced perspective requires your team to acknowledge that you will have setbacks and disappointments. It also encourages the golden-lining view that collectively you can and will vanquish them. Realistic, proactive, and positive applications of correct principles provide the means. When implemented, the balanced and appropriately optimistic perspective enables a more thorough long-term pursuit of purpose.

—CUE CARD—

BALANCE THE ORBIT

SEEK AND PRIORITIZE
A BALANCED, REALITY-GROUNDED PERSPECTIVE

Result: Balanced and grounded perspective gives the big picture view to enable adjustments and adaptability toward increased productivity.

Team Benefit: Seeking and prioritizing perspective sets the stage for the highest team-member engagement.

Crew Notes for Business Execution:

8	Balance in viewpoint, effort, and attitude within a team optimizes performance.
7	Attempt to keep the tone light and positive, even when dealing with serious team and project issues.
6	Proactively including humor and conscious breaks in the normal activity flow serves as a "pressure-relief valve" and is a wise investment of time and effort.
5	Life's too short to die all tensed up. Cultivate among the team the ability not to take things personally.
4	Humans are naturally resilient. Amplify that quality in the team with backup approaches, allowing team control of as many aspects as possible, and maintaining a realistic view of challenges faced.
3	Encourage fitness and promote wellness. Individual and team productivity will benefit.
2	Don't sugarcoat reality, but don't let it scare you off either.
1	People who exercise "golden-linings" optimism realistically acknowledge the difficulties ahead, yet with a balanced perspective, confidently realize that they can diligently overcome the obstacles.

Spaceflight Example: Psychologists have coined the term "overview effect" after studies of astronauts' and cosmonauts' changed viewpoints from having seen planet Earth from an off-world perspective.

TETHER TO PRINCIPLES

7

"On matters of style, swim with the current; in matters of principle, stand like a rock."

—President Thomas Jefferson

Purposeful Performance Principle 7: Adherence to values-based principles prevents drift and systematically keeps execution on track during preparation, action, and follow-through.

Leaders must follow and teach correct principles to avoid drifting away from mission accomplishment. Constant assessment, as guided by key principles, limits errors in strategy and tactical execution. It requires discipline, constant attention, and astute prioritization.

Limit the Drift
A final, gentle swoosh of air shoots out as the airlock finishes repressurizing. Our two spacewalking crewmates, Linda Godwin and

Rich Clifford, have just completed a six-hour extravehicular activity (EVA). Not just a casual stroll, the two spacewalkers had scampered all around the payload bay of *Atlantis* and up on to the *Mir* space station, to which we were docked. The primary objective, which they completed exquisitely, had been to install an experiment package on the outside of the *Mir*, known as the *Mir* Environmental Effects Payload (MEEP). It was an important engineering study to characterize the environment around the space station in terms of orbital debris, micrometeorites, thruster firing residue, and so forth. The results were to fold back into the design of the International Space Station.

As we opened the inner airlock hatch and Rich and Linda removed their helmets, I could see ear-to-ear grins plastered on sweat-soaked faces. Everything had gone perfectly, and the hundreds of hours of training in the water tank and vacuum chambers had paid off handsomely. Rich regaled me with his description of the experience. No matter how stupendous the view from within the shuttle, once outside it, the only thing between you and the entire universe is a single panoramic faceplate. The phrase "overwhelming view" takes on a whole new meaning in this context. I had to salve my little twinge of jealousy with the personal reminder that as a pilot astronaut, spacewalking just wasn't in my job description. On the other hand, from time to time, I got to actually hand-fly the spaceship, as when we eventually undocked from *Mir*, so I had no shortage of gratitude for my own role and experiences.

Regardless of how exciting or intoxicating the spacewalking experience is, though, it is always a critical, high-risk operation. For a safe and successful spacewalk, astronauts apply the principle of "tether protocol." Dual metal tethers secure the EVA crewmember to the structure. Spacewalkers must never unclip both at once. Movement is methodical and careful while always watching the security of your tethers. To let yourself become detached from the vehicle structure and drift away could easily prove fatal.

Tether protocol protects and gives confidence. Should you momentarily lose your grip, tethers limit drift. They anchor you to the structure and are potential lifesavers. Tethers allow you to return to the spacecraft and task if you do drift off. Likewise, those who intentionally tether themselves to correct principles will limit the inherent drift off track. Your team should use your principle tethers to keep pulling you back to all the elements required for successful execution. Values-based principles need constantly to come to mind and guide everyone's actions.

It's impossible to overstate how much more effective leaders are who stay close to correct principles and actively use them to guide their team's plans and actions. Every chapter in this book begins with a key Purposeful Performance Principle. It's also important to highlight the nature of the first principles approach and mention a few additional ones that are important for team execution success. Much like a countdown consists of so much more than the last ten-second verbalization, these and your own additional guiding principles must also contribute.

Start and End with First Principles

We need to always keep our foundational guiding principles in mind. A first principle is the distillation of a fundamental truth. In the formal world of logic or the sciences, such a concept cannot be deduced from any other proposition. It is axiomatic, relies on no assumptions, and does not arrive from analogies or comparisons.

I was fortunate early in my Air Force career, prior to attending pilot training, to complete my graduate studies at the California Institute of Technology. After a very practical engineering program at the Air Force Academy, I found myself thrown into a much more theoretically oriented environment. Even majoring in aeronautics, I don't believe I ever did a single aircraft-specific engineering analysis while there. Instead, the syllabus required starting from essential first principles, such as conservation of mass and energy, to derive a detailed understanding of fluid physics problems.

Not destined to become a Nobel Laureate like a number of brilliant Cal Tech graduates or professors, I was ecstatic just to survive and graduate! No worries, though—I was destined for the operational world of military flying, not a research lab. However, the discipline of constantly forcing myself to break down every technical problem into its fundamental first principles and then build back up to a solution has proven invaluable in a lifetime of problem-solving jobs. Moreover, that first-principles background and approach has often led to my best leadership contributions within widely varying team settings.

Do you thoroughly consider the foundational elements upon which you can assemble success in your endeavors? We normally start much higher up in the process, thinking through analogies or "what worked before." Methods such as mental modeling processes described in the chapters on preparation and awareness do, of course, belong in our teamwork toolbox. However, we also need to expend the intellectual energy to determine what key underlying principles will best steer our team's execution.

You don't need to obsess with a strict definition of what constitutes first principles. Leave those mental gymnastics to philosophers or research scientists. In business teams, though, you absolutely must roll in a strong emphasis on the main elements that will positively drive your results. Wise vision, mission, goal, and objective development should rely on that foundational buildup. Also, in the execution heat of battle, remembering and applying additional axiomatic bits of wisdom will keep you on the success track.

The remainder of this chapter presents a few more fundamental principles universally applicable in team settings. Consider how you can use them as a leader and expand their applicability to your own teams. Then take your own deep dives into the depths of discovering and applying additional specific root principles applicable to your situations.

Constantly Prioritize: Aviate, Navigate, Communicate

Military pilot training is a cultural adjustment for sure. Taking inexperienced young twentysomethings right out of college and tossing them into the unforgiving world of flying jets requires some serious mental reformatting. Part of that process is morning "standup."

Picture this: 0400, 4:00 a.m. in civilian parlance, in the dark of an Arizona morning. Everyone is in place to be ready for the first "go" right at dawn. Still shaking the sleep out of their eyes, student pilots and instructors jumpstart their morning with coffee and donuts. The flight commander arrives and gets right to it.

"EP [Emergency Procedure] of the day is Engine Fire on Takeoff. Lieutenant Searfoss, what do you do?"

I stand up and recite the prioritization mantra drilled into us from day one: "Sir, I maintain aircraft control, analyze the situation, and then take appropriate action." We're also taught constantly to "aviate first, then navigate, finally communicate." I list by memory the critical, immediate-action, "boldface" steps of the emergency procedure. Then I pull out the checklist and continue, asking at appropriate points about what indications I see. Our flight commander responds with more information; then I continue enumerating every consideration and action. Finally, the scenario plays out, and the mental model jet is safely shut down on the ground.

Every single day, every student pilot is on the hook. If you blow it during your turn in the barrel of standup, then you're grounded for the day. Screw up too often, and it could mean no graduation, no wings, and your dream over. Standup is, however, a small price to pay for the incredible privilege of piloting the hottest aerospace machines around. The process is also extremely effective in teaching one to internalize prioritization skills.

The typical work environment is, and should be, less structured and formal than a military pilot training setting. Nevertheless, leaders certainly must demonstrate their own strong prioritization skills. The team will get results by starting with the end in mind and diligently focusing on execution via the PAPA process, which the next six chapters will outline.

Everyone should constantly ask, "Are we focused on the right thing, right now? If not, how do we reprioritize?" Rather than "aviate, navigate, communicate," your own prioritization mantra for a sales team, for example, might consist of "prospect smartly, engage enthusiastically, ask and close!" The specifics of such a short and sweet reminder are up to you and the team and will vary widely. Align it with your objectives, and you'll have a powerful tool to generate focus.

Establish Clear Rules of Team Behavior and Performance

Of what type of team would you rather be part? One with a very strict, even unforgiving, culture but with crystal-clear standards and organization? Or would you prefer a muddled, confused, opaque team where you never quite know where you stand? True performers will always opt for the first.

Of all the factors that cause frustration and hinder execution within a team, the lack of clear expectations ranks among the worst. In fact, in polls of what makes a bad work environment, the majority of respondents consistently indicate that lack of clear direction produces the most dissatisfaction. Preventing that shortfall is one of the first orders of business in building a team.

Leaders should ensure first that overarching company strategy, policies, and guidelines for externally directed team engagements are well disseminated. Additional team-developed "Rules of Engagement" serve valuable roles in defining specifics of internal interactions. These guidelines outline the how, when, where, and what of connecting together to do the joint work. Additionally, in establishing these ground rules, discussion and consensus within the team will guarantee stronger understanding and acceptance. While the formal leader may provide guidance and counsel, team self-direction in establishing these standards is the most effective.

Once established, constant reminders of expectations need to become the norm. It's certainly not just the leader's responsibility. Well-formed and cohesive teams find all members willing, even eager, to uphold the jointly created team rules. Developed and positively promoted, such measures are not constraints. People in strong teams perceive high standards as special elements that allow them to focus and set them apart from less capable teams.

Value the On-Scene Person

Delegation, trust, reliance—all are related elements of valuing the person who is in the trenches getting the job done. The core of the confidence to trust and delegate is a value-oriented perception of others' capabilities and intent. High-trust teams require this perception of the unique value and contribution potential of every member.

This principle is an easy one from which to drift unintentionally. Even in strong teams that conceptually get it, the temptation exists to offer a bit too much over-the-shoulder appraisal or unneeded help. Don't micromanage. Let your teammates astound you with competence and solutions. Legendary World

War II leader General George S. Patton counseled, "Never tell people how to do things. Tell them what to do, and they will surprise you with their ingenuity."

At the end of my second mission, we had to spend an extra day in space. Weather across all of central Florida was horrible. A small tornado had even ripped through the town of Cocoa Beach a few hours before our planned deorbit. Nonstop thunderstorms blanketed the primary landing site at Kennedy Space Center. Of course, we were ecstatic! All we needed to do was change a few configurations on board *Atlantis* and open the payload bay doors. Then we could hang around enjoying weightlessness and the majestic views for another twenty-four hours until we could try again. Space shuttle crews absolutely adored "waveoff" days.

Reopening the orbiter payload bay doors after a waveoff was required to allow the radiators lining the inside of the doors to operate. The separate launch and reentry cooling system worked very well, but was only designed to provide four hours of cooling capability. Although the door opening procedure was easy, if the doors were to jam, you were in a world of hurt. Accordingly, we took it slowly and methodically, carefully observing alignment and status of all the latches and motors. Think of unzipping a jacket very slowly and prudently if you're concerned about the slider catching on the cloth around the track, and you get the idea.

As we joyfully started the door opening procedure to prepare for our bonus space day, we were quickly taken aback. Two of the redundant "talkback" indicators showed that we had a latch that would not release. Had the hook actually been stuck, continuing to drive the door could have jammed it and possibly burned out the motor as well. A door hard-jammed partially open was not a survivable reentry configuration, so it really mattered. Stopping the procedure, we pulled out the binoculars to get a better view of the latch at the aft end of the payload bay, sixty feet away. We on-scene folks unanimously agreed that the latch hook had fully released from its roller and it would be no problem to drive the door. No real concern on our part.

On the ground in Mission Control, a different story was unfolding. In fact, so we later heard, quite the scramble was winding up. Engineers that they were, the mission controllers relied heavily on data. In fact, a noted NASA flight director saying is, "In God we trust. All others bring data!" The telemetry told them we would not be able to open those doors. What turned it into a scramble was the pressure that the only emergency landing option within the four-hour cooling window would require a deorbit maneuver, or burn, in just twenty minutes. In the flight director's mind, he was on the verge of having to make one of the most critical emergency decisions ever in the Space Shuttle Program.

We repeatedly told Houston it was a spurious reading, but it took some real convincing on our part to get them to concur that we could safely drive the doors. Ground insisted that one of us reenter our Spacehab module in the aft end of the bay and peer out its sole porthole located fortuitously about five feet from the seemingly balky latch to verify its status. Our commander, Kevin "Chili" Chilton, assigned me to head back and take a close look. I immediately zoomed from flight deck through middeck, airlock, and down the tunnel, like a guy shot out of a cannon, popping open multiple secured hatches on the way. As I peeked out the window, I saw the latch was completely clear and informed Chili. He was then finally able to give our ground support team absolute confirmation and a nice warm, fuzzy feeling.

In human spaceflight operations, Mission Control normally has incredibly deep insight into systems status. We rightly rely on them to take care of the vehicle and us. In this case, though, one human eyeball was worth more than all the fancy instrumentation and telemetry. The same principle applies to your operations. In every undertaking, place full reliance on the person at the front line with the direct observation and understanding of the situation. Help each other out, provide the backup and encouragement, but also let the line operators fully contribute. Give complete support and credit to the ones in the arena. Leaders, trust and back up your people.

One last note: unbeknownst to us in space, the one available emergency landing site in our time window was Hickam Air Force Base, collocated with Honolulu International Airport, Hawaii. Once everything settled down and we opened the payload bay doors, we learned the flight director had been seriously considering sending us there. It almost made me wish I'd reported back from the Spacehab module that the latch was a no-go for door opening. It would've been an interesting first to land a space shuttle in Hawaii, not to mention we would have been right in place for the perfect post-mission vacation! I wondered: would someone have draped leis around our necks after we disembarked from *Atlantis*?

Rivals Can Become Partners

Shifting business environments, continual mergers and acquisitions, the little fish getting swallowed up by the bigger—never before has the pace of change in the marketplace, in any industry, been faster. Although potentially confusing or disconcerting, these realities also offer new opportunities for creatively partnering and building fresh, mutually beneficial alliances. The principle, more important now than ever, is that companies and teams need to stay sensitive for opportunities to forge new alliances. These evolutionary shifts in the matrix to the nth power sometimes even include groups that have been direct competitors.

The principle also applies to individuals within a given group. Particularly in highly competitive organizations, friendly or perhaps not so friendly rivalries occur. Even within such hard-driving cultures, however, the wise, team-oriented individual will look for the chance to strengthen jointly beneficial partnerships. Step outside the "me-first" zone to the recognition that building alliances relying on one another's particular strengths is a hallmark of effective teams.

When I was a young fighter pilot stationed in England in the early eighties with my colleagues facing the "Red Horde," never did I imagine that in my lifetime I would actually work directly with Russians in a cooperative venture. Yet a scant dozen years later, there I was, on board the Russian space station *Mir* after we docked *Atlantis*. As we participated in a joint mission, I was sharing the spaceflight experience with two cosmonauts, a former Russian fighter pilot and his engineer crewmate. How did such a shift come about? What lessons does this experience bring to the perhaps less politically driven but still important creative business partnerships required now?

First of all, the conditions had to be right. The fall of the Iron Curtain and the precipitous shift away from communism set the stage. Next, it took a trigger. In this case, the trigger was the US government's desire to convince the Russians not to sell hundreds of millions of dollars of weapons technology to Third World nations. So instead, we used our space program as an instrument of foreign policy, proposing a new partnership to work together in space, including an initial four hundred million dollar payment for Russian-provided services.

Those first efforts at partnering led to the Shuttle-Mir Phase One program, where we, tentatively at first, developed the possibilities with the Russians. Throughout the International Space Station Program, the collaboration continued to grow and mature. Even with recent challenges in relations between the two nations, this joint space partnership continues at the working level as a superb, productive exchange.

With today's business environment and global economy, the stage is more than ever set for all types of organizations to partner and creatively, courageously, and proactively pull the trigger and get things moving. Although we will always foresee some of the near-term benefits, invariably, once strong partnerships blossom, unforeseen, serendipitous advantages often dwarf the opportunities perceived originally. If the Russians and Americans can go from cold war opponents to space frontier partners, think of the possibilities for your team.

Fess Up When You Mess Up

Mistakes are forgivable. Hiding them is not. We have to reinforce this principle constantly within the team. It can be tough to admit our shortcomings. Leaders must model the behavior, always following up with how we'll avoid the mistake next time in order to keep getting better. The only way to enable learning from mistakes and then move forward is to transparently present them for dissection and correction.

A pattern of continual blunders in judgment or execution demonstrates an inability to learn from mistakes, so it is far less tolerable than the occasional candidly admitted error when falling short of an ambitious objective. Furthermore, no team should ever stand for a member who regularly covers up even small mistakes or just once hides a big one. Such conduct is pernicious and one of the most destructive degraders of team trust. Relentlessly discourage the behavior. Moreover, for the good of the team, purge the individual who over time continually refuses to exercise the necessary candor. Leaders, this imperative is one that may require great moral courage. If necessary, do not shirk from the duty for the sake of the rest of the team and the mission. All team members and your stakeholders are counting on you.

Astronauts, particularly pilot astronauts, in some sense fly and live in a fishbowl. Coupling that unwanted attention when performance is less than perfect along with the natural human desire not to look stupid can make it tempting to brush aside the fessing up if it seems plausible you could get away with it.

I know of two similar flight operations cases involving NASA pilots who, at low speed, barely departed a prepared runway surface away from home base in a T-38 jet. Now that little T-38 lands very fast, doesn't have anti-skid protection, and can be a real handful stopping on a wet, slippery runway. I'm glad a runway departure never happened to me, but I did have one or two "whoa, Nellie" landings in my career that got my attention! I understand and empathize with the predicaments my two colleagues faced.

The notable difference in the two incidents was the pilot response after the fact. One individual ran out of pavement on a wet, slippery runway and came to a stop in the gravel overrun. He immediately shut down the aircraft to avoid sucking debris into the engines, then had it towed to a hangar. He admitted his mistake right up front, calling back to NASA Aircraft Operations, then waiting around for a day while NASA sent a maintenance technician out. The technician thoroughly inspected the aircraft, particularly the landing gear, engine intakes, and front faces of the engine compressors. He determined it was safe to fly so the pilot departed for Houston. Other than some good-natured ribbing and debriefing by the Astronaut Office during our safety meeting, that was the end of it.

The second case played out differently. Pressing just beyond aircraft crosswind limits, another pilot landed and then found he had just a bit too much sideways drift. He ended up barely coasting off the side of a runway onto a rougher surface containing scattered loose stones that could've damaged the engines if ingested. Powering back to the runway, he taxied to parking, had the jet refueled, and then came home without informing anyone. What he did not realize was that the control tower had reported the incident to NASA. Invariably, living in the fishbowl of being a high-flying astronaut in the white-and-blue hotrod, the word got back to the bosses. It did not end with good-natured teasing, but instead, some significant negative career consequences.

Regardless of how high profile your team activities are, we all face the temptation to brush the dirt under the rug. Don't do it! Momentary embarrassment is always less painful than when intentionally hidden lapses catch up to you and come out. There's great value in collectively recognizing your imperfections, admitting them, and then redoubling the efforts to get better. Leaders, constantly reinforce a learn-from-mistakes culture. Diligent execution means doing a lot, and in taking many actions, we will make errors. It is in admitting and fixing the errors that we execute far more powerfully than if we paralyze ourselves into inactivity for fear of making mistakes.

Tether yourself and your team to the principles of admitting your mistakes, seeking new partnerships, relying on frontline people, and prioritizing wisely. These principles will have positive career and life impact. Furthermore, proactively seek to discern and follow other specific first principles in your organization and industry to keep from drifting off into dangerous territory. Exercise the self-discipline to stay connected to all your most important, values-driven principles. On a spacewalk or the walk through life and the workplace, the tether protocol of tying your actions to correct first principles will protect you and your team.

—CUE CARD—

TETHER TO PRINCIPLES

> ### *ADHERE TO*
> ### *VALUES-DRIVEN PRINCIPLES*

Result: Adhering to principles prevents drift away from mission accomplishment.

Team Benefit: A principles-driven approach sets high standards and keeps the team on track during preparation, execution, and follow-up.

Crew Notes for Business Execution:

7	Tethering to principles protects, adds confidence, and limits effects of errors.
6	First principles incorporate foundational truths and key elements that will positively drive results.
5	Constantly prioritize and evaluate if the team is focused on the right thing, right now.
4	Establish clear rules of behavior and performance within the team. High standards with complete buy-in are hallmarks of effective teams.
3	Delegate and rely on each other. Value the on-scene individual.
2	Keep an open mind, as rivals can potentially become partners.
1	Freely admit mistakes. Never hide them. That's not only a lost learning opportunity, but is also a trust killer when the story eventually comes out.

Spaceflight Metaphor: Spacewalking astronauts always keep one of their two tethers attached to the spacecraft to prevent drifting away and potentially dying.

PART IV
PROGRAM: THE WHAT, WHERE AND WHEN

Program is where the rubber meets the road—team execution. One might term it process, procedures, action, movement, operations, or the daily grind. Regardless of terminology, this category encompasses all that your team has to do—in sweaty, involved detail— to achieve success. Execution counts; results matter. All other categories eventually lead to program. Even while executing daily, the effective team will continually crosscheck and align with purpose, strengthen people, and refine perspective.

Starting with a concept of Objective-Centric Operations, the six ensuing chapters follow the PAPA Effective Execution System I developed. Thinking of this model as an orbit, it is a descriptive and predictive process for execution fundamentals categorized into Preparation, Awareness, Persistence, and Accountability. Refer back to Figure 2; it depicts all the elements of this model, how they are related, and which chapters address each.

Three main features of using this approach apply. First, central to the orbit are specific, actionable objectives. Metaphorically, these objectives are the home planet, Earth. Next, each of the four PAPA categories reside in orbit in alignment with the objectives. These elements are like satellites, held in correct alignment just as the Earth's gravity holds the moon or manmade satellites in their proper places. Finally, leaders repeatedly transit the orbit and rendezvous with the satellites of Preparation, Awareness, Persistence, and Accountability, constantly applying the execution principles within the six program chapters. The pace at which you repeatedly complete the orbit reflects your speed of execution.

The foundation for the synthesis of the PAPA Effective Execution System comes from nearly thirty years of experience in very dynamic team environments. The framing comes from extensive study and preparation for the many hundreds of corporate teamwork and leadership speeches I've given in the past ten years. Then the finishing work comes from the enlightening conversations I've had with a multitude of clients from virtually every industry. Specific tactics and techniques within and across Preparation, Awareness, Persistence, and Accountability, exercised at the optimum pace and aligned with objectives, guarantee effective execution.

6 CREATE OBJECTIVE-CENTRIC OPERATIONS

"A small body of determined spirits fired by an unquenchable faith in their mission can alter the course of history."
—Mahatma Gandhi

Purposeful Performance Principle 6: Achieving correctly defined, well-developed, and suitably emphasized objectives empowers the team to fulfill the mission, turning vision into reality.

Objective-Centric Operations are the home planet in the middle of the PAPA execution orbit, lit and warmed by the sun of purpose. Every execution action should align and focus on accomplishing a necessary and specific key objective. Leaders must ensure prioritized achievement of the right objectives to lead to mission success.

A Rocket Scientist's Vision

Dr. Robert Goddard, inventor of the liquid-propellant rocket engine, was far ahead of his time. Working on the family farm on October 19, 1899, as a seventeen-year-old, he climbed a tall cherry tree to trim some dead limbs. He described the experience thus:

> It was one of the quiet, colorful afternoons of sheer beauty which we have in October in New England, and as I looked towards the fields in the east, I imagined how wonderful it would be to make some device which had even the possibility of ascending to Mars. I was a different boy when I descended from the tree from when I ascended for existence at last seemed very purposive.

Goddard, imbued with a creative, long-range vision and burning with purpose, embarked on a lifelong mission to understand and create the real means to accomplish that dream. However, he wasn't just a fuzzy dreamer, but a quintessential physicist and engineer operating at the leading-edge of his day's technology. He coupled the visionary and purpose-driven life with solid know-how and hard work. With this dual approach, he produced a multitude of astounding operating inventions.

Dr. Goddard's 214 patents include numerous firsts. He invented and flew the first liquid-fueled rocket (dubbed *Nell*), proved that rocket engines produce thrust in a vacuum, first flew a rocket faster than the speed of sound, and developed many other guidance, control, and propulsion innovations.

In his day, many viewed Goddard as a crackpot as he developed and advanced a technology that obviously would never have any practical use. In 1919 he published a book called *A Method of Reaching Extreme Altitudes*. This seminal work described his previous extensive experimentation and gave theoretical explanations to illustrate the potential of rocket propulsion, including the prospect of targeting the moon. The reactions ranged from skeptical to cruel mocking. On January 13, 1920, *The New York Times* issued a scathing and technically very flawed editorial berating Goddard and stating, "Of course he only seems to lack the knowledge ladled out daily in high schools."

How did Dr. Goddard react to the criticisms? He replied, "Every vision is a joke until the first man accomplishes it; once realized, it becomes commonplace." Furthermore, the words from his high school valedictorian speech in 1904 proved prescient: "It is difficult to say what is impossible, for the dream of yesterday is the hope of today and the reality of tomorrow."

A scant thirty-three years from the March day when Dr. Goddard launched *Nell,* the Soviet Union did exactly what he had proposed and *The New York Times* had mocked. The *Luna 2* probe escaped Earth's gravity, made it to the moon, and was intentionally crashed into the lunar surface. The Soviets, and the Germans before them in World War II, had diligently studied Goddard's work. Competition driving us, eventually America captured the vision and had humans riding rockets by 1961. Within the decade, Apollo 11's lunar module, *Eagle,* soft-landed on the moon, forty-three years after *Nell's* 2.5-second flight.

By the way, on July 17, 1969, the day after the launch of Apollo 11, *The New York Times* issued a short article under the headline "A Correction." This piece summarized the 1920 editorial along with an updated conclusion: "Further investigation and experimentation have confirmed the findings of Isaac Newton in the 17th Century and it is now definitely established that a rocket can function in a vacuum as well as in an atmosphere. *The Times* regrets the error."

Dreams to Reality

Robert Goddard serves as a superb model for choosing to do hard things with a grand vision and pursuing them with an unquenchable sense of purpose. As his inventions and patents testify, he and his teams also set a compelling example in completing the concrete, real work to produce operating hardware. Goddard, certainly a dreamer and visionary, was also a practical doer. And his work really was rocket science, made all that more difficult because he pioneered the way as one of the very first in this esoteric field.

The literature and experts generally correlate conceptually on definitions of vision, purpose, mission, goals, objectives, and the like. Subtle yet significant differences in approaches do exist. The emphasis in this book is more on tactical execution with purpose, versus these more strategic activities per se. Now, with Objective-Centric Operations as the central planet of the PAPA orbit, comes the point where strategy and tactics converge, with the development and application of pertinent objectives.

My most compelling observation of hundreds of organizations with which I've worked is that the more intellectual and emotional investment leaders and teams make in transferring high-level strategic concepts into actionable objectives, the better they create the conditions for ultimate success. Doing the conceptual work up front to craft and internalize the big picture direction is necessary, but not sufficient. We need then to follow up with the steps to actually launch on a workable vision-to-reality trajectory.

Purpose gives the "why." Vision and mission highlight the future-state, strategic "what" and "who for." But these overarching concepts need to flow down into the concrete "wheres, whens, hows," and detailed "whats" of goals and objectives. Dr. Goddard's teams most assuredly worked from wisely crafted goals and detailed objectives to chart the flight path from rocket dreams to hardware reality. Likewise, our teams need to make the transition from conceptual to concrete to continue toward execution success.

As we approach liftoff, it's time to address how to establish and meet goals and objectives. To achieve goals, we must take tangible actions with diligent concentration, each developed with clear, specific objectives in mind. Properly formulated goals and central objectives establish the route toward effective operations that actually get productive work done.

Flowing to Goals and Objectives

Actions matter! Migrating from longer-range abstractions to the real work takes work. To fulfill vision, mission, and purpose, your teams have to get progressively more dialed in. The team must flow its understanding and documentation down into ever more detailed goals and objectives.

Most people do not differentiate between goals and objectives, and in many applications, the distinctions are moot. But for involved, complex undertakings in today's business environment, it is crucial to pin down the differences to define the optimum pathways to real achievement. While goals and objectives both support mission accomplishment, goals are broader, less specific, and less imbued with numbers and performance metrics than objectives. Both, like vision and mission, require considering the "what." Rather than dwelling only on the desired end state, goals and objectives consist of shorter-term building blocks. In every case, you should be able to make a clear link showing how meeting an objective or achieving a goal will contribute to fulfilling your mission.

It is acceptable for a goal to be a little softer and less specific than an objective. Using descriptive words versus actual measurements and framing them as narrative milestones is effective. Going back to the Neurolab example, the science mission of "going to outer space to explore inner space" required multiple goals. These goals described the essence of safely and efficaciously completing primary neuroscience experiments, numerous secondary studies, and assorted engineering test profiles. Progress toward accomplishment of those goals began years before launch with selection of twenty-six primary in-flight experiments out of nearly a hundred proposed by research institutions and universities around the world.

Objectives absolutely must plunge even more deeply into the practical pool of specific actions, accountability, numbers, and measurement. In addition to the "what," they positively must directly address "where, when, who," and often "how."

For one of the primary Neurolab experiments, scientists were trying to learn why astronauts developed peripheral circulatory control problems while they were weightless. Is the brain not issuing the correct signals to the veins in the legs? Is the nerve traffic suppressed? Are the veins just not responding? To move beyond the essential goal of successfully completing this experiment to having a solid plan to do it proved extremely difficult. Our science team considered it the single most challenging physiology experiment ever attempted in space. The scientists and managers worked and reworked multiple supporting objectives. It eventually all came together with the necessary procedures, equipment, and contingency plans to make it actionable and achievable.

Objective Specificity: A Little Microneurography, Anyone?

Big word, microneurography. Don't worry because you'll get the pilot's explanation! This high-priority experiment required literally wiring into the vagus nerve, which runs up the outside of the leg, to measure the tiny electrical signals transmitted from the brain to control peripheral circulation. Meeting the goal of completing this experiment necessitated many underpinning objectives. Each objective, in turn, required action and accountability from team members. For the inflight data collection, our crewmate Dr. Jim Pawelczyk, astronaut and eminent researcher in his own right, was to collect X readings for Y minutes each of vagus nerve signals and other bio data from Z subjects in microgravity at various intervals throughout the flight.

Many people in the broad team had to collaborate to meet the goal of successfully conducting the study, but only specific individuals could do certain things. Objectives, because of specificity, require actions from distinct individuals. The principal investigators with whom we worked came up with the hypothesis to be tested, developed the hardware, and trained us. Only we astronauts could perform the experiment in space. Furthermore, Dr. Pawelczyk was one of the top five experts in the world most proficient in performing microneurography, so he did the vagus nerve probing.

Jim poked and prodded others of us as the test subjects. Even there, in development of the objectives, the desire to gather as much data as possible bumped up against constraints requiring detailed and time-consuming consideration. For operational safety reasons, NASA Safety would allow neither CDR nor PLT to be in-flight test subjects in the very restrictive microneurography test apparatus. Should an on-orbit emergency arise, it would cause too much delay for Scott or me to get free, zoom up to the flight deck, and handle the problem.

Though desirable from a data perspective, operational safety requirements precluded having a needle poked into my nervous system while in space. Darn that luck. However, as described previously, for certain leadership example reasons of my own, I did volunteer for this particular invasive experiment pre- and post-flight, when the safety restrictions did not apply.

The STARS Approach to Defining Objectives

Numerous guidelines exist to help teams zero in on results-driving objectives. If you have already embraced one or more, you're clearly on the right track to producing the right type of operations you need for success. My own research and practice in many team ventures through the years has produced my favorite five areas for emphasis in objective development. Being a space guy, I've rolled them into the **STARS** acronym.

Objectives must be **Specific, Timelined, Actionable and Accounted for, Realistic,** and **Sensed.**

Specific. The detailed "what." Also the "where." Sometimes guidance on the "how." Make it concrete! Abstractions will only dilute effort. Again, goals can be a little bit broader. Objectives must get down to the details. Think of a funnel with a wide opening of vision, mission, and purpose, then narrowing down to goals, and finally, at the very bottom, objectives. This neck of specificity forms the last part of a progressively tightening structure that sends the work down the chute for action.

Timelined. The "when." Two elements of time matter. First, create a challenging deadline to build the sense of urgency and emphasize the importance of the objective, then lay out the schedule. Parse out how much of that critical resource of time it will take. In orbit, astronaut crew time is a critical and limited resource. Every human space mission operates with a detailed "timeline." For some events, like initiating critical maneuvering thruster "burns," timeline precision to the second is required. For housekeeping activities, like vacuuming dust off the avionics filters, "sometime during the day" works. Regardless, the time element of objective accomplishment is always considered.

Actionable and Accounted For. The "who." State your objectives such that someone must actually do something. The very act of writing the objectives using active voice and plenty of verbs helps. When you couple an actionable event to an accountable person, the conditions exist to "make it so." Early in my military flying career, I had a superb operations officer. Our squadron worked like a fine Swiss watch, at every level and with every tasking. His secret: "belly buttons!" For anything that needed doing, he insisted on "a belly button to push if it's not happening." He made the tasking objectives crystal clear, looked his chosen responsible person in the eye when he made the assignments, and expected results. By the way, with that clarity, he rarely needed to push on any belly buttons! These days, of course, literally pushing on belly buttons is not a wise action to take in the workplace, but figuratively, it's a superb idea.

Realistic. The team needs to choose consistently challenging individual objectives. At the same time, though, rely on the team's collective wisdom and expertise to define the boundaries of what is doable legally, morally, physically, and financially. A test to know if you're on track for an attainable yet challenging objective: it gives you just a little feeling of nervousness in the pit of the stomach, coupled with an excitement and anticipation to get to it. Team consensus is very important during this step. A healthy respect for all opinions and constructive conflict in frank discussions will really hammer it out.

Sensed. As in measured, numbered, or counted. Performance metrics complete the package. The metrics should be as analytical and quantitative as possible. Use of the word "sensed," however, also allows room for the idea of noted but not necessarily fully measured, as in sensed intuitively. The objective has to pass the overall common sense "smell test." Early in my flying career, I had a wise instructor tell me, "Rick, when you walk up to the jet and something just doesn't smell right, get to the bottom of it before you go fly." In other words, rely on your experience to fill in subtle gaps where the analysis might not show the whole picture. Trust your gut as well as your data. Being a Spider-Man fan growing up, I tend to call it my "Spidey sense." When the Spidey sense tingles, pay attention!

Crucial but Not Direct Objectives

The Neurolab microneurography case study describes just one of hundreds of detailed, thoroughly developed objectives that flowed up to a lesser number of more general goals of one particular Spacelab science mission. In addition to these goals and objectives, such a complex undertaking required multiple less direct, but still essential, goals and objectives too.

For example, safely landing *Columbia* supported all the science on Neurolab but was not a primary mission goal. It's hard to evaluate the science if it doesn't return unharmed. Worst case, if the commander had a really bad day flying any given space shuttle landing, it could have resulted in loss of orbiter, crew, and payload. Fortunately that never happened. Significant resources and training time were always devoted to making certain the CDR could meet the stringent landing performance objectives. Details of that level of preparation make for an interesting case study themselves and will be addressed later.

Obviously, a safe return to Earth was a necessary, though not direct, goal of the mission. Landing is the end of the commute, yet not the Mission that Matters by itself. Think of the types of activities your team must accomplish in its overall workflow. Some will lead right to the bottom line and address the main mission. Other factors, such as maintaining the team itself, anticipating future trends and changes, and even mundane activities such as setting up physical office space, may not be quite as direct. Concentrate on identifying which ones are crucial, even if not direct, and craft solid STARS objectives for them too.

What's a Commander to Do? See the Trees *and* the Forest

Thousands of people worked to prepare and execute any space shuttle mission. Only a relative few, however, had a complete understanding of how it all fit together. The commander and the flight director were primary. Other big picture team members included the mission manager and payload manager, each with a support staff to do detailed planning. Lab flights also required another crewmember to serve as payload commander to cover the multitude of very specialized and detailed science requirements. Rick Linnehan, the only other veteran on STS-90, served in that role for us.

Even in the midst of my own intense and time-consuming training prior to STS-90, I always thoroughly enjoyed my regular tag-ups with these other "see-the-forest" folks. Most of them had been working the flight preparation longer than I had, with invaluable insight. Their contributions were essential. Each understood all the nuances of the mission, what the goal priorities were, and how to craft and track the hundreds of detailed objectives—the trees, so to speak—to meet those goals. Working together in close communication enabled us to make tradeoffs, reprioritize as necessary, and continually refine the preparation—all very necessary groundwork to lead to smooth execution.

In addition to the weekly meetings, Rick Linnehan and I constantly compared notes. As we traveled extensively for training and meetings around the country, Rick usually flew in my T-38 backseat so we could effectively use the en route cruise time to discuss mission objectives and crew training. As productive as the time was, however, the talks weren't always entirely mission related. Once, at forty-one thousand feet, somewhere over west Texas, we were chatting about how we both grew up in New Hampshire. Noting that we had attended neighboring high schools and graduated just a year apart, we figured out that "back in the day" we had actually played soccer against one another for our respective schools! What are the odds?

Everyone on the team needs to maintain awareness of goals and contribute to defining and executing objectives. Designated leaders have the additional responsibility to step back often, take a broader view, and weigh the goals against one another. That prioritization enables them to adjust objectives appropriately and reassign resources as necessary.

Learn from Having to Adjust Your Objectives

"OK, Searfoss, the Wing Commander is flying with us tomorrow, and he's going to be on your wing. Weather's supposed to be good up in Scotland, so get together with your WSO to start planning the route. We've got Rosehearty Range scheduled for you after the low-level. Briefing's at zero seven hundred. Questions?"

Just one, I thought. *Why me?* I was a brand-new flight lead, barely a junior captain. How did I draw a "chance to break even" straw? Colonel Bracken was a no-nonsense fighter pilot and warrior with 130 combat missions, most over North Vietnam flying the F-105 Thunderchief. He would be watching every single thing I would do, from flight planning, through my briefing, and during an intense, nearly three-hour flight. He had a fierce, objective-centric orientation when it came to his crews hitting targets accurately and on time. "No questions, sir. We'll be ready."

After a focused afternoon of planning and an evening of studying, my WSO and I felt pretty set. Like preparing for a final exam, though, I still had some nagging doubts. No matter, I knew I had to give the assignment my best shot. The next morning the briefing went fine, no problems getting airborne together, and I didn't do any stupid flight lead tricks like abruptly turning into my wingman as we transited up to Scotland though the murky English clouds.

We dropped into the low-level environment a couple hundred feet above the beautiful southern Scotland countryside. As pre-briefed, once below the clouds, "Dash Two," the colonel, automatically moved out to a mile-line-abreast tactical spread. I began to push it up to nearly six hundred miles per hour. I was feeling good. *Target, here we come*, I thought. My objective was in mind. I was focused.

And then, "Ba-boom!" The loud bang was followed by some whimpering, grinding noises. All the left engine instruments rapidly wound down. Immediately, the day's objective changed from hitting the target to getting the jet on the ground in one piece. Good thing the Aardvark is a two-engine beast, or it would have been ejection city, because that engine was down for the count. No longer the least concerned about the target, I was way too busy securing the engine via the correct emergency procedure, popping up to get some altitude, and calling Scottish air traffic control: "Pan, pan, pan, *Vark Zero-One*, F-111, request vector to nearest suitable airfield."

The military controller, in his calm, Scottish brogue, immediately responded, "Roger, *Vark Zero-One*, fly heading three-four-zero, Leuchars [a Royal Air Force base] thirty miles on the nose."

"Two, drop in and take a look, I think we had a turbine blow up." I continued to work the emergency procedure while turning for Leuchars. "Looks clean and dry, lead." The colonel had shifted from commander evaluation mode into fully supporting his junior crew in returning a multimillion dollar Air Force asset safely to the ground. Just prior to landing, following the single engine approach, everything copasetic, Colonel Bracken departed my wing with a hearty, "Great job, Captain. See you back at the 'Heath." He had changed the nature of his support in flight because circumstances conspired to prevent meeting the original objective. A few days later, after a maintenance crew came up to Leuchars and replaced the bad engine, I flew the jet home.

The day after returning home, my squadron operations officer informed me, "Captain Searfoss, Colonel Bracken wants you to come up to his office and debrief him on your engine failure." I wasn't so nervous this time. I knew I'd done a good job with the emergency and that he knew it too, and I very much looked forward to the interaction. I gained far more than I expected, though, during that exchange. He provided a memorable and lasting leadership example after I debriefed him.

Ed Bracken took the time, one on one, to give me some wise counsel. In congratulating me for handling the emergency so well, he strengthened my confidence. He then reiterated how important it is to quickly shift gears, reprioritize, and adapt when it's obvious in real time the original objective has to change. As our discussion wrapped up I mentioned that I hoped to eventually become a test pilot. Colonel Bracken then gladly offered to write a recommendation for me for the day when, with substantially more experience, I would apply to Test Pilot School. He mentored, encouraged, and developed his subordinate while recognizing my future potential.

Clarity and Focus: The "Too Bad" Rule

Within a couple months of launch, all space shuttle crews were absolutely buried with details. The work week progressively expanded to as much as one hundred hours, counting study time. Sometimes, the many support teams seemed to offer too much help. For example, it was not uncommon to return from a few-hour training session to see on your desk a four-inch stack of new paperwork containing procedural changes and corrections awaiting your immediate review.

From my previous experience, I knew that excessive time spent with such administrative reviews could distract us from the true training objectives. The process required every single in-flight procedure change, even typos, to undergo crew review. The forms directing such changes were called "483s." Late in a training flow, 483s could prove the bane of a crew's existence.

At this point, you were out of time and brain space for anything but objective-focused training. From my experience, I made a command decision for my Neurolab team that everyone really welcomed. Two months prior to launch, I initiated the "too bad" rule when it came to 483 paperwork: Make a quick overview of each pile as it comes in. If it is safety-critical or a crucial procedural fix, spend some time reviewing it. Otherwise, kick it back with a smile and a note that says, "Too bad I don't have time for this one." Then, simply let the system implement it or not. We had to maintain laser-sharp focus on our clear and present objectives of getting ready to fly the mission.

As transition from strategy to tactics, Objective-Centric Operations prepares the way for effective actions. Remember that the real world will constantly conspire to confuse and complicate everything the team plans and does. You fight back using the clarity and prioritization that solid, pertinent objectives provide. Concentrate on establishing that clarity with STARS objectives. Maintain process integrity and discipline in laying them out. Arm yourself against incoherence and confusion that the hectic, complex business environment introduces. Clear objectives will defend against distractions and provide the needed focus during execution.

—CUE CARD—

CREATE OBJECTIVE-CENTRIC OPERATIONS

> ### DEFINE, DEVELOP, EMPHASIZE
> ### SUITABLE AND CLEAR OBJECTIVES

Result: Defining suitable objectives transitions strategy to tactics to turn vision into reality in fulfilling the mission.

Team Benefit: Clear objectives empower the team to meet its purpose.

Crew Notes for Business Execution:

7	A vision is at best a dream, at worst a joke, until someone actually accomplishes it.
6	The trajectory from dreams and hopes to reality requires carefully crafted, focused, and pertinent goals and objectives.
5	Goals and objectives both address the "wheres, hows, whens, and whats." Objectives, however, are more specific and data-driven than goals.
4	STARS Objectives: Specific, Timelined, Actionable and Accounted for, Realistic, and Sensed.
3	Consider also the crucial, but not direct, support objectives.
2	The designated leader must constantly prioritize, weigh goals and objectives against one another, and encourage everyone on the team to contribute to that effort.
1	Concentrate on establishing clear, focused objectives. Maintain the discipline to stick to them and to defend against distractions.

Spaceflight Metaphor: Progress toward objectives mirrors the trajectory after launch—onward and upward toward rendezvous with targets and success.

PACE IT PERFECTLY

"Diligence is the mother of good fortune."
—**Miguel de Cervantes Saavedra**, from *Don Quixote*

Purposeful Performance Principle 5: Pushing ahead diligently, with a long-range view, opportunities orientation, and optimal pace, fosters the responsiveness to stay ahead of problems and competitors.

L
eaders need to demonstrate a strong sense of purpose-driven urgency, coupled with the seemingly contradictory ability to look ahead and think long term. Execution focus requires sensing the right pace, pushing beyond the status quo, and driving change as needed. Creative ideation, opportunity focus, and rapid development leverage leader-inspired optimum pace for results that count.

Time to Come Home

It's reentry day. The payload bay is all buttoned up. We've stowed everything not absolutely required. The flight deck and middeck seem virtually empty. Our spaceship is nice and tidy. Once suited up in the bulky orange pressure suits, we astronauts floating around inside *Columbia* resemble the bloated helium balloons of Macy's Thanksgiving Day Parade. Soon all seven humans take their seats, four on the flight deck and three downstairs. We strap in, knowing that, for this mission anyway, the free-flying weightless feeling is behind us. Granted, we and the seventy earth-pounds of suit, helmet, gloves, parachute, life raft, and more are still weightless for a bit longer. Nevertheless, the five-point harnesses hem us in, as if spider webs have captured seven fat caterpillars. We won't be getting out until on Earth.

I execute the deorbit burn, simply pointing the spaceship backward and firing the six thousand-pound-thrust orbital maneuvering system (OMS) engines for a few minutes. Then I fly it back around with a pure pitch maneuver to place the pointy end first, using the much smaller Reaction Control System (RCS) thrusters. It's very straightforward, so I'm not feeling rushed. Afterward, we're still moving nearly five miles a second, or 17,500 miles per hour, but now we've lost barely more than one percent of that speed. It's enough to start descending and heading home.

Ironically, as fast as we're still moving, we humans are now enjoying a very sedately paced interlude. It's close to a twenty-minute freefall until we begin to encounter any atmosphere, with nothing to do but monitor flight path and systems and wistfully ponder our departure from this magical realm. The flight deck group has time to gaze longingly out the window, knowing that those magnificent views will soon no longer be possible. That's already over for the folks in the middeck. The three of them have to stare at a bank of off-white middeck lockers from now until flight's end. It's a very calm and relaxing time, quite unlike every simulation where we would be working multiple emergencies and scrambling to keep up with everything going wrong.

Even after we hit Entry Interface (EI), there's still nothing dramatic. Only our instruments tell us we're now in the atmosphere. Gradually, *Columbia* starts to slow. We know all that energy has to go somewhere, and a few minutes later, at about Mach 17, seventeen times the speed of sound, we begin to see where. The brilliant light show begins. The pinkish-orange, two thousand-plus-degree plasma screams by the window just a few feet from my head. There are dramatic flashes and glow, sure, but my workload's still pretty reasonable, and we're all very comfortable.

Screaming east over the Pacific, we encounter a brightening, rosy dawn, then go "feet dry" over the California coast just before nine in the morning local time. Now it's less than twenty minutes to run until touchdown in Florida. We are flying the same ground track that our STS-107 colleagues, also on *Columbia*, will follow on their ill-fated reentry some five years later. For us, *Columbia* perfectly, automatically, and majestically S turns back and forth to precisely control her trajectory. Out the side cockpit windows, Scott and I drink in astonishing panoramic vistas of deserts, mountains, the southern plains, farming country, forests. That screaming, hypersonic "low-level" across America the Beautiful is a first for me because my previous two flights had landed at Edwards Air Force Base, California. Breathtaking!

The more *Columbia* slows, the more actions we need to take. No more time to gaze out the window. Even without emergencies like in the simulator, the workload ramps up noticeably. Rather than operating off a timelined schedule like in orbit, the PLT and CDR flip switches and do their work based on Mach number, our speed relative to the speed of sound. Also, throughout the entire reentry, we constantly monitor flight path, energy state, and all the vehicle systems.

Mach 7: check our navigation system status and update the computers if it's good. Mach 5: deploy the air data probes and evaluate the readings. Much earlier and the metal probes would've burned off—not a good thing. Mach 2.7: several actions must take place, including turning on our heads-up displays (HUDs). Landing coming up soon. Busier and busier, but in a groove from countless hours of training.

Over north Florida, we're three times higher than commercial airliners fly, but we're only a few minutes from touchdown. A crystal-clear midday Florida sky lets me see the Shuttle Landing Facility about a hundred miles southeast. Soon, it's time to turn off the autopilot. Deep breath, focus, and hand-fly this two billion dollar beauty just like I've done over twelve hundred times before in the Shuttle Training Aircraft (STA).

Work pace is a fast run now, but still measured and controlled. So much going on. Stay ahead of the aircraft, or in this case, winged spacecraft. Scott Altman, awesome crewmate that he is, supports me magnificently every single step of the way. Kay Hire pitches in perfectly with pertinent information as trained and briefed. The docs quietly enjoy the ride while pulling for their aviator teammates. All the training is paying off.

After I take over the maneuvering from the autopilot and begin hand-flying, the next few minutes pass in the blink of an eye. It's a marvelous feeling to see the actual runway line up directly under the outline symbology on my HUD as I roll out on high final at twelve thousand feet. We're in a cognitive sprint now, with every single second full of pertinent actions, communications, and crosschecks. Before we know it, it's time for the gear to come down. Next, we're over the threshold in the last airborne mile of our six-and-a-half-million mile flight. Not that we have the slightest inclination or moment to look, but we could've spotted our families and NASA support personnel watching us from a few hundred feet away right abeam the approach end of the runway.

Absolutely every single second of the previous hour had flowed exactly as planned and practiced. The process, training, and our own diligence had brought us safely together to this point. We hadn't had to fight any gnarly problems. I had *Columbia* in the groove, set for the heaviest space shuttle landing ever and ready to touch down on the Shuttle Landing Facility Runway 33. It was still too early to celebrate, though. The task was not quite over. The objective was still unmet, so concentration was at its peak. Then, with *Columbia* about five feet off the ground, from both left and right seaters came minor exclamations of "What's that?!"

"That" was an unexpected and significant wind side gust that bobbled *Columbia*. With my hyper-acceleration-sensitive middle ears from sixteen days in space, I instantly felt as if I had been tilted beyond ninety degrees to the left! Nothing else to do but just hold what I had and let her touch down ever so slightly sooner and faster than desired. Everything was well within limits, but not quite perfect. Derotation, rollout, and drag chute deployment were uneventful. Finally my call to MCC, "Houston, *Columbia*, wheel stop." We were home, and I was still a bit dizzy from our little gust encounter.

Postflight analysis showed that it was the highest instantaneous wind gust that any landing orbiter had experienced. A single, minor "unknown unknown" had had an impact. Although the landing was well within limits, the perfect touchdown had eluded me. For an obsessive technical perfectionist, frankly, that was a bit disappointing. Nevertheless, the training, execution, and pace had come to fruition. Ken Cockrell, a fellow classmate in the 1990 Astronaut Group, congratulated me on the mission a day later. He added impishly, "The solid, within limits landings are what we train for. The perfect ones take that plus a little luck. Still a great mission!"

Commute though it was, bringing *Columbia* home on landing day was a crucial operation that required total focus and excellent pacing in its completion. Getting "behind" the spaceship could've proven disastrous. The preparatory approaches were long term, recognizing that there are no easy solutions or quick fixes. This team had to evolve to that precise, stay-ahead-of-the-spacecraft level of execution while also anticipating possible glitches or upsets. The process for any opportunities-oriented team moves from handling "messy" ideas and uncertainties, to consolidating and refining until reentry day, and finally to completing the mission.

Look Out a Few Galaxies Distant

The Hubble Space Telescope gathers in the faintest of light that has, in some cases, traveled for nearly thirteen billion years, crossing unimaginable distances. It's the ultimate in the long-range view. In its twenty-five years in space, upgraded and improved during five shuttle missions, it has produced a stunning scientific and visual bonanza for humankind.

My Neurolab crewmates Rick Linnehan and Scott Altman went on in their astronaut careers after STS-90 to visit Hubble. Scott commanded the last two Hubble servicing missions, and Rick served as a spacewalking telescope maintenance man. With tremendous pride in my former crewmates, I followed those missions with great interest. During Rick's mission, I considered an interesting contrast.

For Rick to successfully complete his three servicing spacewalks, he had to execute perfectly, in the moment, second by second. His world during the total twenty-one hours of those three EVAs was very short-term oriented, with focused attention to every single detail. Rick himself likened doing those servicing spacewalks to completing surgery on a whale, another moment-by-moment, skillful operation he has done in his veterinary career. Out of nearly seven billion humans on the planet, he's the only one to have had those two particular, diverse life experiences! Contrast that intense, short-term focus with billions of years of photons zipping across the universe to impact on Hubble's mirror to produce the images of its most distant observations.

Of more direct applicability for execution pacing are the human scale, long-range elements that have given us the phenomenal science and ethereal beauty of Hubble's imagery. Even the very concept of sending to space an astronomical observatory of such size and capability took a very long, visionary view. After more than a decade of development, launch finally came, only to discover a heartbreaking myopia due to a two in a thousand aberration in the original grinding of the telescope's mirror. Patient persistence through repair allowed us to reap the scientific bonanza. Designed from the outset to be upgraded and modernized, the Hubble Space Telescope has since lived a long and extremely productive life.

In team execution, the long range works its way down progressively to smaller chunks of time of prime concern. It had taken years to plan to the second every motion and action for a Hubble spacewalker, with months and months of dedicated training to rehearse. The long range flowed to the short term and bore the fruit of successful execution.

Even in the midst of hanging in there day to day, team members need to consider longer time frames. The operational relevance of the high-level vision, mission, goals, and objectives spurs that mindfulness. The objectives serve as regular reminders of just where the team needs to head, allowing current actions to align with the desired ends. A key execution leadership function is to remind people continually of those objectives. In parallel with a long-range future view, a rearwards, history-perceiving outlook is also valuable. Winston Churchill said, "The farther back you can look, the farther forward you are likely to see." That occasional rearview mirror glance, however, is only useful if done with an earnest desire to extract and apply lessons learned. Playing the "woulda, coulda, shoulda" game pays no dividends. However, thoughtful analysis of where and how mistakes were made will clarify what must happen for success going forward.

Expand your view of the timeline, both forward and backward, even if not to thirteen billion years. The effort will give you and your team a more thorough understanding of how your work and challenges fit together. Applying that insight at successively more detailed planning and activity levels helps meet the day-to-day demands of execution.

No Quick Fixes

Orbital drag is extremely weak, but it is relentless. Most people don't realize or care that it even exists. At low Earth orbit altitudes, a couple hundred miles up, the vacuum isn't quite complete. Even at that height, a few atoms per cubic centimeter of monatomic oxygen and other elements zip through the ether. If you're out there in your spaceship, the widely spaced atoms constantly pepper you. It's actually enough to exert a pound or two of force on the football field-sized ISS. With the constant, though weak, degradation, the station must occasionally re-boost its orbit. Flight controllers constantly pay attention to how much the orbit degrades and fix it when needed.

Likewise, subtle daily drag chips away at you and your team. Whether it's "Murphy's Law," a myriad of little seemingly unavoidable delays, or just fatigue, the drag continues endlessly. Countering it takes ceaseless patience and an acceptance that it will be a continuing, ongoing battle.

With the ever-accelerating pace in business today, it is important to address problems quickly. Time pressures can tempt us to reflexively slap a Band-Aid on issues and move on. While quickly dealing with problems makes sense, rushing to a hoped-for solution does not. Instead, it is better to dig down to root causes, let everyone on the team have a say in proposed actions, then implement solutions carefully. This approach may require extra work and team multitasking, but it is more comprehensive. It takes patience, but when things get fixed, they stay fixed. In the long run, the patient, comprehensive style proves more efficient and effective.

Sometimes, we also fall into the trap of thinking that if we have a standard procedure for a given issue, we'll simply follow the steps and work our way out of it just fine. Just because you're following a defined process does not mean you can put your brain in hibernate mode! Continue to question while implementing. Be prepared to go beyond the process. Bottom line: don't consider a problem solved until it truly stays solved long term.

Breaking new ground in technology, particularly rockets, is not for the faint of heart. In aerospace development, physics just won't let you cheat. It takes time, and reality is hard. XCOR Aerospace is on the verge of realizing a fifteen-year dream as we build the Lynx suborbital spaceplane. Even as technically proficient as the team is, no one thought it would take so long. The deeper you go in such an ambitious, never-been-done undertaking, the more you uncover, the more you have to solve, and the greater the real-world difficulties. With patience, uncovering and then solving one technical issue after another, the real flight hardware is coming together.

As XCOR's Chief Test Pilot, the plan is for me to be the first to put the Lynx through its paces. I'm often asked, "So, Rick, when will it fly, and when will you be going back to space?" The answer is always, "When it's ready!"

Work hard; work quickly; but to do a job right, don't count on quick fixes.

Start with Messy Ideas

Staying ahead of your spaceship as a performance competency means that once execution begins, you have the preparation, pace, and skills to implement the plan while dealing with the inevitable delays and "what ifs." Long before then, though, every initiative and significant teamwork package will have gone through a development process. How that process starts will ultimately contribute to how well it ends and how far ahead of the game the team stays.

The journey from initial concept to precise execution can start messy. That's fine, even preferable. Messy ideas are the first fruits of our creative impulses. The crisp, "Roger, Houston, we'll put that in work," implementation of a finely honed plan never starts out that way. It's an evolutionary process.

When you're exploring and researching where no one has done something before, you absolutely must start with an open mind. Get the team comfortable with uncertainty. Embrace the unknown. Explore various idea pathways in the initial idea development brainstorming process. Early, nonjudgmental presentation and discussion of ideas is a valuable process. The team should set aside definite blocks of time to do the open-ended group thinking, promoting everyone's thoughts and varying ideations. Continue to challenge assumptions, redefine parameters, and reinvent approaches. Synergy comes from the "riffing" on one another's ideas.

You do need to limit the process in some dimensions. Two effective ways come to mind. First, block a specific amount of time for the evolution. Messy ideation can be mentally taxing even to the most out-there thinker, and it helps to know a given session won't drag on endlessly. Next, limit each session to just a few key issues or challenges (two or three only). Strictly adhere to topic discipline, even appointing a session referee, if necessary, to keep everyone on task.

Many more tools exist for a group's early-idea development. Research this topic and assemble a full toolkit to take creative ideas up higher and higher rungs on the development ladder. Eventually the team will have numerous initiatives at various stages. The ones near the base of the ladder may be fuzzier and less defined while more refined ideas will fill in the top levels. Suffice it to say that the messy start is usually a necessary precursor to the eventual smooth-as-silk precision execution.

Opportunities Orientation

Orbital sunrises are achingly beautiful. In the span of just a couple minutes, the view goes from velvet darkness, scattered with untold pinpoints of light, to a brilliantly illuminated jewel of a planet below. In seemingly the blink of an eye, the sun first starts peeking through the thin line of the atmosphere, transits it, and pops out the other side, much whiter and starker looking than the yellow ball we see from Earth. During that brief transit, its light produces a constantly varying, multihued array of crisp, delightful color splashes and reflections on your spaceship: vermillion, fuchsia, auburn, ochre, magenta, and every other exotic hue imaginable. Glorious!

Astronauts love to float in the flight deck during a sunrise, or the nearly as stupendous orbital sunsets, to revel in that breathtaking beauty. You do have work to do, however, and often duties keep you downstairs or in the lab without the panoramic windows. It's OK, though. With one orbit every ninety minutes, you have sixteen opportunities per day to see an orbital sunrise or sunset. The key is to recognize the opportunities are there, stay aware and sensitive to them, and then capitalize when possible.

Business opportunities present themselves the same way. Everyone has to stay on the lookout for them. The leader needs to make such scanning a very high priority in his or her crosscheck. Furthermore, when everyone on a team takes the same approach, it becomes a huge execution excellence multiplier. Opportunities are out there, whether "the next big thing" or the countless small, mundane improvements to the business you can make. The team that stays heads-up and on the lookout will be that much farther ahead in capitalizing on them. Everyone on board needs to develop the confidence to see challenges less as problems and more as chances to achieve even greater things.

I met original Mercury 7 astronaut Deke Slayton a few weeks after I showed up for initial astronaut training in 1990, less than two years after we had returned to flight after recovering from the *Challenger* tragedy. Although retired, Deke still lived in the Houston area and stayed abreast of everything going on with NASA human spaceflight. He discussed, perhaps with a wish to climb back aboard himself, how it was a very exciting time in the program.

Deke went on to show his opportunities orientation. With a backlog of a wide variety of very demanding missions, he indicated our class of sixteen mission specialists and seven pilots had tremendous possibilities ahead of us. Then he confidently expressed his opinion that we would complete training splendidly, seize those opportunities, and contribute markedly to America's human spaceflight goals. His confidence and outlook truly inspired me. I was walking ten feet off the floor. I never lost that opportunity-perceiving viewpoint I gained from one of the original astronauts.

An opportunities orientation reflects the abundance mentality that *7 Habits* author Dr. Stephen R. Covey expounded. The more the team can conceptually expand the size of the pie, the more filling, or seized opportunities, can fit into it. An optimistic, though still realistic, look at their operating environment—an opportunities-oriented viewpoint—does not, unfortunately, tend to be a natural inclination for most people. It takes work and conscious effort to scan the horizon with that mindset. As we refine the ability, however, it does bump the team execution pace up to a higher level. We metaphorically stay further ahead of our spaceship.

The "So What?" Question

Most people, if asked what goes into the making of a test pilot, might imagine the derring-do days of years gone by when a bold soul strutted out to a brand-new machine, just hopped in, and went. If he survived, he became a test pilot. It has never really been that way, even in the old days. The year-long, formal test pilot training conducted for more than sixty years at a handful of professional test pilot schools worldwide is much more comprehensive and structured.

In fact, I found the most challenging part of completing the US Naval Test Pilot School was not the flying at all. Instead, it was refining the ability to evaluate dispassionately, even while perhaps in the middle of a wildly gyrating spin, and then succinctly communicate the assessment. Mandatory follow-through to that evaluation, imperative for the engineering test pilot, is expressing the relevance of your observations and data. It's one thing to get numbers. It's an entirely more subtle and demanding requirement to relate the data to an aircraft's mission.

The one bit of advice that really broke the code for me was when one of my instructors counseled me always to ask about any observation, "So what?" Example: The airplane rolls too slowly. "So what?" The pilot will then have problems lining up precisely on final approach. "So what?" In high crosswinds or with a narrow runway, he might land off to the side. "So what?" He could damage or destroy the aircraft! OK, now we're getting to the relevant root of the issue.

A pretty simple process really, but it has a way of focusing your thoughts. That focus, in turn, will help you dig down to the essence of whatever particular problem you're working on. Unearthing the core issue or "mission relation" will help you get out ahead of your challenges, carving out more time and brain space to solve them. Try it out. Do your own test flight of the "So what?" question with whatever's vexing your team. It will serve you well.

Finally, Pace Yourself

A very fine line separates maximum performance from being out-of-control. Flying a high-performance jet fighter just within the bounds of its envelope is exhilarating and rewarding. Great fun! The fun can end very quickly, however, if you take it just a tad too far, particularly down close to the ground, which wins 100 percent of the time. Playing that fine line well is vital for leaders too.

Pushing hard is important in building the necessary momentum for optimum performance. The key word is optimum. Pushing beyond the peak can become counterproductive, exhausting, and draining. For the leader, it's more art than science and requires constant attention. Get out on the floor, sense the energy levels, and talk it up with your team. Take a well-deserved respite at completion of breakneck-paced projects. Pull out of the fight temporarily, if necessary. Renew to get your "smash" back up, then come roaring back into the "furball!"

Often, you have to slow down to speed up. Mindful, purposeful progress consistently pursued beats sprinting, followed by gasping inactivity, almost every time. We all know the story of the tortoise and the hare. In space, that way of working makes even more difference because it's so easy, physically, to make inefficient, useless motions as you attempt to work.

Rich Clifford, my STS-76 crewmate, was the absolute master of efficiently extracting the utmost in useful work out of his activity in space. With him there was no wasted effort, just elegant motions and complete focus. The man never got behind on his timelines. At first glance, it appeared he was just casually drifting through space, but it was invariably with an unequaled economy of effort. Although I was no rookie either on my second spaceflight, working with him and observing his purposeful way of living and working in space improved my effectiveness.

Drive the team toward efficient and productive activity. Constant mindfulness of what you're doing keeps the wasted effort to a minimum. If certain activities aren't measurably contributing to accomplishing objectives, just stop doing them! Breathless pace doesn't mean you're necessarily ahead in the race to achieve the actual objectives.

You don't have to be fully ready until launch day. You'd better be making steady progress all along, but perfection does not come overnight. Work steadily, managing time as a valuable resource. You've established the framework earlier in this countdown in doing the up-front mission definition and objective development work. Coupling that with building a trust-based, prepared, and aware organization, your balanced, principled team can execute effectively at the right pace.

—CUE CARD—

PACE IT PERFECTLY

> ### PUSH AHEAD DILIGENTLY
> ### ON PACE, WITH LONG-RANGE VIEW

Result: Pushing ahead diligently maintains positive progress to stay ahead of problems and competitors.

Team Benefit: Perfect pace fosters team creativity and generates an opportunities orientation.

Crew Notes for Business Execution:

7	Total focus and excellent pacing does not happen by accident.
6	Drive toward highly anticipatory outlooks with a long-range view. Simultaneously evaluate and learn from the lessons of the past.
5	In reality, there are no true quick fixes. Even while working quickly and efficiently, recognize that there are no shortcuts to doing the job right.
4	Start with messy ideas, then massage, develop, and rework them into operationally useful solutions.
3	Look at everything with an opportunities orientation that then grows to develop a team abundance mentality.
2	Constantly ask the "So what?" question. What's the relevance; why does it matter; how will it affect the outcome with respect to meeting objectives?
1	Pace yourself and the team. There's a fine line between maximum performance and being out-of-control. The intent should always be to optimize overall performance.

Spaceflight Example: Landing the space shuttle is one of the most critical, fast-paced team operations possible, enabled through the right preparation, training, and attitudes.

PREPARE DILIGENTLY
AND CONSTANTLY

4

"By failing to prepare, you are preparing to fail."
—**Benjamin Franklin**

Purposeful Performance Principle 4: Deep preparation and guarding against complacency in planning, training, and briefing accelerate the team into effective action.

R elentless preparation lays the foundation for all actions that will produce successful execution. Leaders must constantly fight organizational complacency and inspire team members to prepare continually. It takes diligence and an unremitting desire to keep getting better. Making the necessary sacrifices to prepare unceasingly reflects the depth of commitment to the team's highest purpose.

A Great Day to Fly, or Not

Another beautiful day to fly. Off for a great low-level mission through the mountains of southern Idaho. What could be better? Cleared for takeoff. Run up the engines and light the afterburners. Accelerate down the runway. We can't wait to get airborne, sweep the wings way back, and light our hair on fire screaming around at near supersonic speeds two hundred feet above the deck for the next couple hours.

Break ground, up come the gear, on comes the red left engine fire light. Whoa, that's different! In twelve hundred hours of flying F-111s, that's the first time I've ever seen that come on in flight. Instantly it's **THROTTLE (affected engine)—OFF, FIRE PUSHBUTTON—DEPRESS, AGENT DISCHARGE SWITCH–UP.** Do the immediate, boldface actions and keep flying the jet. It's quite a handful because, heavyweight and single-engine, the Aardvark lives up to its namesake as a real "earth pig."

We've got an experienced wingman right behind to back us up. Get some altitude and airspeed, start bending it around to come back to the landing runway, and watch the light. As we declare an emergency and announce to tower our problem, the light goes out. Looks like the fire is extinguished. Our wingman concurs.

Walk in the park now. Set the flaps only partially down for less drag, and wait to lower the gear until we're coming down glide slope. Gear's down. We're close. Energy is good. Got it made.

Our wingman passes behind us for one last look right before we touch down. "Lead, you're still on fire!" Doh! The procedure says to eject if the fire continues. Everything looks fine in the cockpit. We're a mere few hundred yards from touchdown. I weigh the options and instantly decide we're staying with it, exclaiming forcefully to my right-seater, "We're not ejecting!" He replies, "Roger," and keeps his hand away from the capsule's ejection handle.

I land and immediately get on the "binders," taking full advantage of the jet's heavy duty, anti-skid brakes to screech to a halt. Immediately, I shut down everything. Unstrap, open hatches, and drop to the tarmac. Then it's "runaway, runaway!" Back to high school track days. As far as we know, something is still burning in our not-so-trusty steed. With nearly five thousand gallons of jet fuel in the tanks, it's not too wise to hang around. The fire trucks arrive and quickly secure the situation, giving that jet the chance to fly again.

Our responses had come readily and automatically because of so much study, training, and emergency procedures practice. Preparation, preparation, preparation! Even today, twenty-seven years after my last F-111 flight, I can still recite the engine fire boldface procedure from memory. Although this instance was my first actual inflight fire, it was old hat from the many hundreds of engine fires in the simulator and simulated single-engine approaches in the aircraft. Not much more than another day at the office.

When I got home that night Julie asked me how work went. "Fine," I replied. Then I caught her up on a few things happening in the squadron with people she knew. "Oh, and I had an engine fire today, but it all worked out just great."

"What?! Why didn't you call me right away?"

"Well, I had paperwork to do, and it all ended well, so I didn't think about it."

"Great, but what if I'd heard about it from someone else without the straight scoop? Think about that, OK?" Note to self: *I guess it actually was a big deal. Knucklehead, keep Julie in the loop!*

Will that same deep level of preparation matter for your team success? Absolutely! Nothing else can accelerate you and your team as quickly into truly effective execution. All the preliminaries—vision, mission, building the team trust and competence, identifying clear objectives—provide groundwork. With that foundation, then the further detailed team preparation for execution can begin in earnest.

When you begin to think you're ready, you're not even close. Plan and replan. Leave no stone unturned. Consider all that might go wrong. Rehearse. Keep it simple, executable, and elegant. Talk it up within the team. Finally, iterate. Go back and repeat the process, over and over.

Active, Ongoing Planning

The first key area of execution preparation is planning. Planning initiates preparation. It needs to continue constantly, and the plans themselves should be living, regularly updated tools. You need to roll the most current lessons and adjustments into the plan.

Crucial to successful Objective-Centric Operations is not just the planning, but a vibrant, robust planning process. General Dwight D. Eisenhower, supreme commander and architect of D-Day during World War II, testified, "Plans are nothing; planning is everything." The very exercise of considering all the necessary planning elements, even for the smallest of activities, points you toward success.

Chances are, your company already has strategic planning processes in place. However, it's been my observation of hundreds of organizations in many industries that the closer you get to the operational team level, the less emphasis is placed on a planning mentality. You and your team need to establish and use a focused, tactical planning method, even in the small things, during daily execution. That process must constantly consider what the current objectives are and fully support their achievement.

For regular operational planning, here is a straightforward, five-step planning framework I've developed. It's another STARS acronym: **Scenario, Tasks, Assess, Resources,** and **Steps.**

Scenario. Get everyone's head around what they're facing, whether large and comprehensive, like an annual sales target planning drill, or small and simple, like a schedule of the day's activities. Consider the overall operating environment (the lay of the land). Think about how that might impact what you're trying to do. In a simple example, traffic delays from roadwork between your office and an offsite meeting with a client could set back the entire day's work if not considered. In larger and broader contexts, operating environment considerations could have implications for the very existence of your team.

I recently worked with a company that had just announced a huge joint venture with a larger partner. Once completely merged, the new corporation would form the biggest company of its type worldwide. The leaders were very excited, but also anxiously striving to understand how their teams would fit into the new structure. We pondered all the ramifications of the new environment. Fortunately, the exercise reinforced that as long as the teams continued to deliver similar stellar results, they could confidently plan for a bright future within the new organization.

Tasks. Tasks flow from objectives. What are specific action items you must do within the available time? Carefully define the scope of what you need to do. Understanding of scope will determine the required timeframe and execution timing: when to start, when to expect to finish. Make your best estimate of timelines, then list, in prioritized order, all the tasks necessary to meet given objectives.

Assess. Assess what? Primarily focus on the items that will hinder your objective accomplishment. What are the risks in terms of lost time or money you might face with a given course of action? What are competitors doing? Considering the threats to a business operation, though probably not lethal like in tactical aviation if neglected, should still take a high priority.

Even the regulatory situation needs to be assessed as a potential hindrance. Of course, certain industries, like healthcare, are much more heavily regulated than others. At best, government regulation adds some workload; at worst, it's like operating inside a vat of sticky molasses! Regardless, the team must thoughtfully consider all potential slowdowns or showstoppers.

Resources. Resource consideration involves stacking up what you have available to meet the objective. People, equipment, funds, and other tangible resources typically come to mind first. Also, pay attention to intangibles, such as knowledge, brand strength, goodwill, and intellectual property. We will always want more of every resource since resources generate benefits. With rare exceptions, though, we will always operate under resource constraints.

In human spaceflight history, there's a huge difference between the essentially resource-unconstrained days of the moon race and the more limited funding available ever since. Resource constraints are similar in your world and generally tighter now than ever. Your key is to get the most out of the resources you have, and the first step along those lines is to consider them wisely.

Steps. What specific sequence of actions do you take? Here you roll every prior phase together as you refine process and outline detailed procedures. It's also where the team needs to consider training and education requirements for the people who will do the work. People are your team's most important resource, so the next step in preparation beyond planning is to get them totally up to speed.

Specific and focused training is one of the most underrated and neglected aspects of team preparation in the business world. Considering training upfront in the planning gives it the priority it deserves. Then, after addressing training in the planning process, teams need to devote the time to actually do it.

Skills-Based Training and the Chair-Flying Technique

Detailed training requirements are very industry and situation specific. With that fact in mind, however, some universal considerations for preparation through execution-promoting training still jump out. First, wherever possible, training needs to be skills-based and hands-on. An example of an active, skills-based training program would be an online or in-person role playing sales simulation, allowing application of various techniques and principles. Such relevant practice, instead of a passive lecture, proves much more efficient at preparing new sales folks to hit the ground running. Skills-based training more effectively prepares the learner to engage, do, and act.

During my time in the Astronaut Corps, NASA evolved astronaut training from its traditional, heavily scripted training into a more skills-based approach. It begins in earnest after basic systems study, with a broad exploration of what the vehicle or system can do. Along the way, the learners practice the general skills. Then, over time, they transition to higher fidelity scenarios and then to more specific, realistic actions. By that point, the axiom becomes, "Train like you're going to fly," down to every possible detail you can control.

The Remote Manipulator System (the RMS, or robotic arm) provides an example of skills-based transference. Primarily a system that mission specialist astronauts used, it was not carried on any of my missions. Still, I had a couple of occasions to "fly" the arm in the simulator. The formal training flow built up in very small, specific, numbers-driven increments and was extremely conservative. Once, though, in a "pickup" generic sim with Chief Astronaut Hoot Gibson, I tried out a few maneuvers. Hoot and I were both very experienced radio control model airplane enthusiasts, and he introduced the RMS to me by saying, "Just look at the end of the arm as if it's one of your RC models out there and do what comes naturally." Bingo!

The RC skills directly transferred to operating the arm, and I found it quite natural and easy to do. We then joked that NASA ought to buy some top-end RC models as an introduction to RMS training.

Today, more and more superb training resources in every field are available online. Generally, such online learning programs are skills based, self-paced, and modular. Programs often include strong feedback and practical applications. Search out the ones relevant to your team, encourage their use, and accelerate the pertinent training you'll need to execute at the highest level. As you do so, don't forget another amazing training resource: our minds, especially when using the "chair-fly" technique.

Our thoughts, when channeled properly, have incredible power to self-train us. In flying training, we call it chair-flying. It essentially involves a complete mental rehearsal of a given flight, methodically working through the entire sequence. For best effect, chair-flying even involves moving the hands as if you actually have a stick, throttle, and multiple switches in front of you. I went so far before my first space mission to set up a full-size paper copy of *Columbia's* instrument panel in my home office. My kids laughed at Dad and his toy orbiter cockpit, but it aided my preparation tremendously. Even to the present day, after I've flown eighty-four different types of aircraft, mental simulation is a key part of my preparation in learning a new airplane.

Pacing, anticipation, muscle memory, ability to counter objections or problems, and confidence all benefit from chair-flying. Some learning experts indicate that concentrated, correct mental ideation of performing an event can replicate up to 90 percent of the synaptic connections used in the action. Mental rehearsals, your team's own version of this practice, will hasten team member preparation. These drills are not just for hands-on tasks either. Repeated, concentrated mental simulations will also boost performance presentation skills, making sales calls, you name it.

Execution Preparation Communications: The Briefing and More

Years ago, I ran across a humorous piece comparing fighter pilots to apes. While many similarities do exist, in at least one way the two differ markedly: "Apes almost never brief one another!" The preflight briefing is an essential and never-neglected part of the pilot's world. This briefing is the bridge between preparation and action, crucial for mission execution and safety.

A few years prior to becoming a test pilot, I graduated from the Air Force Fighter Weapons School, a pinnacle, four-month advanced training course for instructors in operational fighter and attack squadrons. The entire program was intense, particularly the preflight preparation and stringent standards for briefings and communications. It was not uncommon to prepare for four hours or more to conduct the one-hour flight briefing. After the flight, our instructors critiqued our briefing effectiveness for another hour or more—even before beginning to discuss the flight execution. We only half-jokingly said that if we could just get through the briefing, everything else was a piece of cake. In retrospect, that intense communications emphasis was spot-on. After all, upon graduation, we would head back to our squadrons as the recognized experts on weapons and tactics and would need to share that knowledge effectively with our colleagues.

Regardless of the industry, your team needs to develop a briefing mindset too. Depending on the scope and scale of any of your team's particular operations, a briefing may be formal, extensive, and lengthy. Or, it may just as easily be a quick reminder chat between two teammates about some of the planned activities for the morning. Taking advantage of technology, people can hold briefings while spread out around the world. Wherever possible, however, the impact of face-to-face connecting is still stronger. The important principle is that, for significant, objective-centric actions, the team needs to connect the plan with the activity. You need to talk about it—and effectively.

Leaders need to highly prioritize effective meetings and briefings. Conduct them yourself or delegate this task within the team. Regardless of who conducts the sessions, always stay focused on objectives, even to the point of explicitly stating, "OK, what we intend to accomplish today is . . ." Organizationally, using the exact same STARS pattern as in planning is not only convenient, but also provides a consistent framework. Brief what you planned! The briefing itself should be structured like a funnel, starting with the big picture and narrowing down to more and more specific aspects.

Sharp execution begins with precise attention to details. Start and end on time. Keep it crisp and to the point. I use what I call the "C4" communications elements to make sure my briefings meet that standard. These execution-directing communications must be "clear, complete, concise, and concrete." Running that phrase over and over in my mind keeps my briefings and other team communications on track. Try it out, not just in briefing, but with any team communications.

Brief to the experience level of your team. The dynamic will vary depending whether you have a group of seasoned veterans running a plan they've done many times before or your team includes less experienced members. Take a little time within the briefing to mentor and encourage those less-experienced folks.

Assign resources and responsibilities to distinct individuals. Going back to the belly button example, the team should have an accountable individual for every single action item it needs to accomplish.

Keep briefings as interactive as possible. The level and type of interactions will vary with the formality and situation. Regardless, everyone on the team should feel he or she can contribute and question.

Finally, great briefings set the tone and build the right communicative team culture. The positive influence of solid briefings extends to all inter-team communications. So don't be an ape. Communicate early, often, and well. A briefing mentality will powerfully help your team do so.

"Specialization Is for Insects": Broad-Based Preparation

A human space mission flight director has to keep the big picture in mind, make the tough calls, and protect the crew and vehicle. Flight directors operate with an overwhelming amount of often conflicting inputs and data, all pouring in from the dozens of Mission Control front-room controllers and hundreds of back-room support engineers. The mental gymnastics, leadership, and communications challenges are formidable. Only the best NASA Mission Operations personnel get the nod to become flight directors. Their intensity of preparation parallels that of the flight crew.

The ascent and entry flight director for my first mission, STS-58, was an experienced Mission Operations veteran named Wayne Hale. Wayne, brilliant technically, also thought deeply about organizational challenges and team relationships. He has many outside interests as well and is quite a renaissance man. Toward the end of our training, as our simulations became progressively more complex and we worked with the entire MCC team, we interacted with him quite regularly.

One day, I attended an ascent procedures review in Wayne's office. My eye caught a poster prominently displayed on his wall with a quote from the great classic science fiction author Robert Heinlein, one of my favorites. I was familiar with the quote, loved it, and was glad to see that it expressed Wayne's outlook too:

A human being should be able to change a diaper, plan an invasion, butcher a hog, conn a ship, design a building, write a sonnet, balance accounts, build a wall, set a bone, comfort the dying, take orders, give orders, cooperate, act alone, solve equations, analyze a new problem, pitch manure, program a computer, cook a tasty meal, fight efficiently, die gallantly. Specialization is for insects (*Time Enough for Love*).

As I grew to know Wayne, it would not have surprised me if he could do virtually all of those things. He's certainly a jack of all trades, plus master of a few very intricate ones. He led his organization with that same philosophy. No cloistered, overly specialized, uncommunicative insects on his team. Unquestionably, his control team was a finely tuned organization, with a powerful preparation culture and deep and broad sets of understanding. I was supremely confident that with Wayne in the flight director position, we astronauts and *Columbia* were in the very best of hands.

Complacency Really Will Kill You

Incomplete preparation and unaddressed shortfalls going into execution indicate complacency. Complacency inhibits the thorough, confident competence required for teams to execute at world-class level. It will suck the life out of an organization and send a team on a debilitating downward spiral. In my business, complacency can literally kill you off as quickly as anything.

With so many hundreds of examples of complacency's negative effects in aviation, let's just consider a few positive ones that show how warding off that complacency ties into preparing a winning approach.

As a brand-new astronaut, it was time to check out in the T-38. These little jets are the same aircraft we Air Force pilots flew in our advanced training. It had been many years, but with all the experience and thousands of flight hours since then, it was easy to think, *How hard could it be?* Well, when it comes to a NASA T-38 instrument flying check, very hard. The NASA mission requires that astronauts travel extensively, night or day, mostly into very busy civilian airports. Flights are often solo into the most congested airspace in the country, with no autopilot to help. With much of the flying between southeast Texas and Florida, you must also deal with some of the worst thunderstorms around. You are extremely fuel limited, with no luxury of time to wait things out or waffle in your decisions. As a NASA pilot, you'd better have it all together in that little jet, or you could find yourself in unrecoverable trouble quite quickly.

Plus, way back in 1966 the Astronaut Corps had learned a very hard lesson. During the Gemini Program, two astronauts, Elliott See and Charlie Bassett, died when attempting a difficult instrument circling approach in marginal weather conditions. Ironically, these astronauts flew into the very building where technicians were readying a Gemini capsule for their upcoming spaceflight. Subsequently, NASA Flight Operations instituted the most stringent instrument flying proficiency standards imaginable.

The performance standards on NASA pilot instrument check rides are the highest I've ever seen in any flying organization anywhere. The mission demands it. Even as a very experienced test pilot going in to that initial NASA instrument check, I took the evaluation as seriously as any I'd ever had. Preparation and never allowing complacency to rear its ugly head enables reaching that apex of piloting performance. It's a great feeling to have such total mastery of any difficult operation that you confidently know you can handle whatever comes your way.

Top team performance in commercial aviation also requires the same rigorous preparation-based culture. Everyone recognizes and applauds Southwest Airlines for its fun-loving attitude. Many fewer people realize that up in the cockpit behind those closed doors, Southwest pilots operate with the strictest discipline in the business. Their company standards far exceed FAA mandates or most other carriers' practices.

For example, approaching landing, when the pilot flying wants the landing gear lowered, it's not, "Hey, Joe, drop the wheels." Instead, it is a crisp, always the same, "Landing gear—down," command to the pilot not flying. Why? It's to develop disciplined, error-preventing habit patterns through diligent practice. Also, on every landing approach, even with a perfectly clear sky, the Southwest First Officer must call out several specific, above-ground altitude milestones. Why? Those seemingly extra calls build over time a complacency-thwarting awareness to prevent smacking into the ground while, for example, handling a distracting emergency on the proverbial dark and stormy night.

Complacency indeed can kill, literally, in any type of aviation. But figuratively, it can also kill off team competency. A striving, constantly preparing team will fight off complacency and prove robust and resilient. Preparation will pay off with tangible results. Leaders, show the way. Do your homework. Leave no stone unturned in your own preparation, and emphasize its criticality to your people.

—CUE CARD—

PREPARE DILIGENTLY AND CONSTANTLY

> *PREPARE DEEPLY FOR*
> *EVERYTHING YOU DO*

Result: Constant preparation through planning, training, and team communications sets the stage for focused pursuit of objectives.

Team Benefit: Diligence up front accelerates the team's ability to actively produce positive outcomes and fight off complacency.

Crew Notes for Business Execution:

7	When you first think you're ready, you're not. Plan and replan. Leave no stone unturned. Rehearse and practice.
6	Actively plan through the second STARS method: Scenario, Tasks, Assess, Resources, and Steps.
5	Effective, business-relevant preparation uses skills-based training supplemented with correct mental ideation.
4	Communications should follow the C4 pattern: Clear, Complete, Concise, Concrete.
3	Incorporate dedicated briefings, also using the STARS pattern, to align planning with team communications. Great briefings set an action-oriented tone and build the right communicative culture.
2	Team members should not only master their own specialized roles, but have sufficient cross-training and broad expertise to effectively back up others.
1	Complacency kills. In your preparation and execution, constantly question, adapt, and never settle for the status quo. Even if it's good enough today, it won't be tomorrow.

Spaceflight Example: On launch day, you absolutely must be 100 percent ready for every planned action, possible emergency procedure, and "unknown unknown." Your life depends on it.

DRIVE AWARENESS
AND LEARNING

"Whenever you are asked if you can do a job, tell 'em, 'Certainly I can!' Then get busy and find out how to do it."
—**President Theodore Roosevelt**

Purposeful Performance Principle 3: Peak productivity takes superb knowledge and competence, strong situational awareness, and a relentless drive to improve.

Constantly questioning, learning, and expanding skills marks high-performing leaders and teams. Such teams enjoy competitive advantages of higher competence and versatility. Integral to such a culture is the almost compulsive desire to continually push for better results.

Innovate, Invent, Showcase

The Experimental Aircraft Association (EAA) AirVenture fly-in and airshow is the largest event of its kind in the country. Each summer tens of thousands of aircraft of all sorts and hundreds of thousands of people converge on Oshkosh, Wisconsin, to celebrate all things aviation. The skies are thick with airplanes coming and going. During AirVenture week, the Oshkosh control tower is the busiest in the world.

I've never done the fly-in thing, taking a little airplane into Oshkosh for the week. And I'm not normally an airshow pilot. I'm a test pilot, nearly as much engineer as stick-and-rudder guy. However, a few years ago I had the chance, as part of a developmental flight test program, to fly as an airshow pilot too.

As a contract deliverable, one of the companies for which I test fly, XCOR Aerospace, needed to make three public demonstrations of a unique prototype rocket-powered racing airplane we had developed. Our client, for maximum public impact, chose Oshkosh for the venue. Unlike all my previous test flights of the X-Racer prototype—out in the California desert, with few observers—I piloted these high-performance flights in front of over a hundred thousand people. What fun!

Showcasing XCOR's technology proved extremely gratifying. Setting up our operation at Oshkosh, preparing the still experimental rocket plane to go, and then lifting off precisely on time for each demo flight required flawless team performance. Flying the bird was thrilling. More importantly, the flights were a culminating tribute to confident knowledge-enabled and skills-driven team competence. I've worked with XCOR for over ten years now and have grown to deeply appreciate the most talented rocket engineers on the planet.

When your team really does do rocket science, a healthy respect for facts and objective analysis must predominate. Actually, we call ourselves rocket engineers at XCOR because it's not really rocket science until you've blown one up! In over four thousand rocket engine firings through the years, including sixty-nine flights on vehicles carrying humans, we've never done that. This team continues to astound me as having the strongest learning culture of any organization, large or small, I've ever seen.

XCOR knows how to develop team competence and awareness. It is the quintessential Learning-Plus organization. The XCOR culture relentlessly promotes discovery, questioning, and experimentation. Working with some of the most exciting technology around, the company is able to hire some of the best young engineering talent in the country. We tirelessly improve technologies and processes with a "build a little, test a lot" approach. Finally, operating in a physically energetic and potentially very dangerous business, our team recognizes that a learning attitude, high situational awareness, and an improvement mindset will protect us and keep our operations moving forward.

The Learning-Plus Team: Pathway to Confident Competence

A team with a strong learning ethos enjoys many competitive benefits. It adapts more quickly and responds more effectively to change. Team members operate with greater confidence and expertise. Complete competence starts with the seed of a curious, knowledge-seeking culture. For maximum business impact, learning must focus on the specific business environment and challenges at hand. Although broadly beneficial, it's not sufficient to promote generic, less directed development and education.

Furthermore, enhanced knowledge is just the start. The sum of individual commitments to soaking up relevant know-how synergistically expands the value of the acquired learning. Free and open crosstalk and information sharing weaves a team learning web. Mutual understanding of different team members' jobs reinforces the web and builds backups within the team.

Leaders should provide as many formal training opportunities for their teams as possible, again keeping in mind that training needs to be relevant and timely. The leader's commitment reflects dedication to building the nodes aspect of the matrix. Everyone on the team should also pay attention to informal training opportunities. Most learning and training comes on the job, informally, through interactions and practice. Willingness to engage in peer coaching leverages that learning tremendously.

Beyond book learning, team members need to earnestly practice skills, both technical and interpersonal. Skills implementation brings constructive action into the learning process. After all, the end objectives in a business setting are never simply to know something, but to act effectively on that knowledge.

Mental Simulations

A few years ago, I read a fascinating study of how operators in complex, rapidly changing, and sometimes dangerous environments make decisions. The book, *Sources of Power: How People Make Decisions*, evolved from Dr. Gary Klein's initial research with firefighters. Subsequently, he expanded his studies to include professions such as critical care nurses, nuclear power plant operators, and pilots. As I read it, I reflected on my own experiences in many emergency situations in high-performance aircraft and spacecraft. Those emergencies included dealing with the only space shuttle ascent hydraulic system leak ever, as described in detail toward the end of the book. Every point Dr. Klein made about the dynamic decision-making process resonated with me.

His essential thesis, borne out with data from extensive research, is called "recognition primed decision making." When it is all on the line without the luxury of time, people quickly classify what is happening into a representative prototype of what they've experienced before. Upon quickly comparing the current challenge to previous ones, operators then identify the first reasonable action that should fix the problem. There is no time at all to think through all the possible options or scribble on a white board while brainstorming. Accordingly, the deeper the well of experience from which to draw, the more likelihood of quickly reaching an acceptable solution.

As astronauts, our learning and training processes subject us to as many off-nominal situations in as high-fidelity simulations as possible. Over time, this process creates a huge reservoir of mental scripts and experiences from which you can draw. A human spaceflight crew has to be a nonstop learning, doing, and mental modeling team.

Your team too can benefit from the same approach. The stronger the learning culture is, the more your team will incorporate vicarious and actual experiences to deal with your particular challenges and opportunities.

Vigilant Situational Awareness

"Don't stow your SA in the map case!" Wise counsel, applicable in many settings beyond just aviation. SA, or situational awareness, is a critical competency valued and emphasized in aviation. The essential principle has long been recognized in military thought, even expressed in Sun Tzu's ancient yet timeless work, *The Art of War*. However, as a specific skill set, situational awareness first took hold within the American fighter aviation world.

Throughout the last forty years, the emphasis on SA has expanded to commercial aviation. In recent years, thought leaders in virtually every industry have also embraced the situational awareness concept. With its wider introduction and attendant detailed academic consideration, its definition has morphed into many varied expressions.

Referring to situational awareness, the academic researcher might use such descriptors as "adaptive behavior," "requires a dynamic task environment," "gives useful knowledge for action," "relates to perception and interpretation," or "lets you understand how events and information will impact accomplishing your goals." However, for practical application in business settings, let's boil situational awareness down to its essence. The straightforward operational fighter pilot would describe situational awareness as simply knowing what is going on so you can figure out what to do next. Everything else is supportive or ancillary.

Situational awareness is one of the plump and juicy fruits of diligent preparation. The incredible teammates I've had in many very dynamic work settings typically started out as naturally high-awareness people. Nevertheless, applying essential planning, training, and communications disciplines, all acquired more robust SA skills. To stimulate impactful execution, you and your teams also need to focus on building that strong situational awareness.

In addition to applying principles already discussed, numerous other techniques exist to bolster team and individual SA. I've always found three particular situational awareness tips helpful. First, simply pay attention to the baseline within your team, company, and industry. Make the effort to stay current. Read widely, focusing on the trends that will impact your business. Sharpen your sensitivity to the subtleties in team relationships. Work at always having a clue! Then when changes pop up, you'll be in tune to the differences and can assess the effects on the venture.

Next, avoid normalcy bias. None of us like to consider unpleasant situations or, in the worst case, disaster scenarios. Normalcy bias is the human tendency to assume that since a given really bad thing hasn't yet happened, it won't. Practice the "what if" questioning. Drive your team to think of dealing with the disagreeable prospects. Fight the tendency to ignore the potentially bad stuff that might be lurking out there. Some psychologists refer to considering and weighing such negative possibilities as "defensive pessimism," though you should engage in the process proactively and with a positive, preventative outlook.

Third, keep scanning. A good pilot constantly maintains a rapid yet accurate crosscheck of myriads of instruments, wingmen positions, threats, target, navigation, and the like. Teams should do likewise. Fight against tunnel vision, or locking your focus onto any one particular issue at the exclusion of other important elements. You must actively balance between appropriate concentration for task completion and "losing the bubble" on everything else. Though this high-mental-energy endeavor is not necessarily easy to do, it's well worth the effort.

Navigation, Guidance, and Control: Iterating to Improve

An important quality for effective teams is to strive ceaselessly to get better. The desire to improve spurs the quest for the knowledge and skills to perform at progressively higher levels. Once up on a given step, the team realizes that with more in-depth understanding, it can and should continue on up to the next plateau. The process is very iterative, and you should maintain the mindset that it never ends.

A space rendezvous and docking trajectory provides a strong metaphor for this principle. We refer to the computers and software that keep the spaceship going in the right direction as GNC components—guidance, navigation, and control. These functions are crucial. Mission Control has a dedicated station with dozens of back-room engineers supporting the primary GNC controller. For purposes of the metaphor, it makes the most sense to present the elements in NGC order. Navigation is where you are now, your current state. You need to make an honest assessment of where the team is, including positives and negatives. Guidance covers where you want to go, your target, along with your desired course to get there. And control is what actions it takes to stay on the desired course. Control represents the detail work of hammering it out daily to produce results, like firing the thrusters to head in the right direction.

A fascinating aspect of GNC on the orbiter is that the equations of motion that the computer systems solve are relatively straightforward, even though the vehicle is moving five miles every second. In fact, because of memory limitations in the ancient 1970s flight control computer technology of the orbiters, the programmers simplified the equations significantly. The key to the technical success in completing a rendezvous or docking with a space station is that the calculations must be constantly updated. I saw that fascinating process play out firsthand as we docked with the *Mir* space station during STS-76. Gaining progressively more precision, in the endgame, we were able to fly *Atlantis* to a docking port with a displacement error of less than an inch at a precise 0.1 +/- .02 feet per second closure rate. Not a bad parking job for a one hundred-ton vehicle! It's all made possible by continually iterating, refining, and improving.

My Bad

Iterating to improve requires finding and fixing mistakes. Often the leader must humbly acknowledge his or her own shortcomings. I have seen many fine leaders model this behavior through the years. Those examples prompted me one day late in the training flow for STS-90 to do likewise. By this time, our crew was clicking together like a well-oiled machine. Our devious training team's job was to throw one emergency after another at us during our simulations. The trainers were finding fewer and fewer ways to stump the dummies. We were on track. As the commander, I was happy, and life was good.

Then came what was essentially the DPS final exam, a several-hour, full-up simulation. DPS stands for Data Processing System, the orbiter's nervous system. The DPS included five GPCs (General Purpose Computers), primary and backup software, and other associated hardware components. The GPCs handled flight control functions and systems monitoring. Those computers were far from user friendly!

In the flight crew, the CDR was responsible for all DPS hardware and software. This particular long simulation started with a scenario in orbit that took out all our computers. Basically, we were dead if we couldn't resurrect them, reload software, realign inertial measurement units, figure out where we were in orbit, update the revived computers, and then successfully transition modes for reentry. This scenario was a nightmare of a training setup, extremely comprehensive, and very painful—but it was necessary.

True confession: I'm a mechanical hardware kind of guy, not a computer geek. I could never get enough of hydraulics or the plumbing of the Reaction Control System. I loved to curl up with main engine manuals. I was always on top of those systems. I thought I was up to par with the computers too—at least going into this evolution. As we plowed through this many-hour evaluation, it became progressively more frustrating. There were way too many rough edges, and although my great crew did fine, I was not at all pleased with my own inadequate performance. Interestingly, our training team lead, perhaps in deference to my seniority and position, politely debriefed the individual items without really brandishing the hammer that needed to fly.

From the training team lead: "So, crew, any last questions?" Well, it was time for me to bite the bullet. I had let down the team, and this had to get fixed. "No more questions, guys, but a comment or two," I said. "My performance was unacceptable. We're going to need to repeat this one. In the meantime, I'll dive back into the books. Please set me up a GPC SST (Single System Trainer) session later this week and a tabletop review with our DPS trainer."

That humbling experience was a great spur. With a renewed interest in becoming a computer geek, I hammered every subtlety of those critical systems into my thick, mechanically oriented skull. A much more confident and DPS-competent CDR led to a vastly better result two weeks later. The second time around it was crew *and* commander finally operating at a ready-to-fly-to-space level.

"Ha, Ha, I Was Here First"

A learning culture helps in processing lessons learned more broadly across an organization. It can't fix everything, but is a good start. The benefits need not be limited to small, operational-level teams either. Sometimes even large bureaucracies can respond with learning-driven course corrections.

In the last few days before a launch, everything rose to a crescendo. It was a busy time at KSC with final preps and checks on the vehicle at the pad, the crew thinking through the upcoming launch, doing final tune-up studying, and the commander and pilot completing one last STA flight. The schedule also included some relaxation downtime at a rustic beach house just a few miles away from the pad. During those times, spouses, accompanied by astronauts chosen by the crew for "immediate family escort" duty, could visit.

After one such visit, our escort offered to take Julie and Cindy McArthur, wife of STS-58 mission specialist Bill McArthur, by the launch pad to see *Columbia* up close. It was the day before launch, and the pad team had just finished rolling back the rotating support structure (RSS). *Columbia* perched there totally unobstructed in all her magnificent beauty.

Stopped just outside the close-in security area, the erstwhile escort, in his blue flight suit and obviously an astronaut, chatted with the gate guard and mentioned he had the wives of the PLT and MS2 with him. The kindly guard said, "Well, in that case, drive on up to the base of the pad to get a closer look." Our escort, fairly new in the Astronaut Office and with no previous experience working at the Cape, queried, "Are you sure that's OK?" The guard's response: "Of course, no problem."

Stepping out at the base of the pad, Julie and Cindy were in awe of *Columbia* looming right over their heads. Another "pad rat" (nickname for launch pad personnel) offered, "Hey, we're between tests up top. Why don't you go on up and show them the White Room?" The White Room is the access area to the shuttle entry hatch, formed on the bridgeway between the pad and the vehicle.

Now little caution bells began to ring inside the astronaut's head: "Can we do that?" The helpful worker insisted, "Sure, as long as you stay with them and check in at the 195 foot level."

So up they went, wives in open-toed sandals, no one having wrapped the required Kapton Tape around watches and rings, female's earrings still in place. They were unknowingly in violation of some important and prudent safety rules. No hardhats either, but that was fine. Hardhats were only required when the shuttle was not on the pad—a risk-risk tradeoff between protecting noggins and a falling hardhat damaging the multibillion-dollar spaceship!

Julie and Cindy got an up-close and personal look that no spouses had ever enjoyed previously. They were blown away by the immensity of it all. Both found it a highlight of their prelaunch experiences and indicated it was a comfort to have that deeper understanding. After all, the next day their loved ones were to cross from that access area onto *Columbia*, possibly not to return home. Cindy and Julie left notes with the White Room personnel for Bill and me to receive the next morning. From my wife: "Ha, ha, I was here first!"

Of course, someone at the pad reported the safety violations, absolutely the correct thing to do. His supervisor called our newbie escort astronaut in to explain himself. Nothing else to do but beg forgiveness. However, in the ensuing conversation, the boss also learned how inspiring and comforting the visit was for the spouses.

An idea was born: Why not lean back into the bureaucracy and build such an event into the plan? Do it right, and future missions could enjoy the intangible benefits for the spouses and, in turn, the crew. So after the obligatory finger wag at our escort, the Astronaut Office engaged in that process and birthed a new tradition. This new tradition was in and of itself certainly no giant leap for mankind. It made only an indirect contribution to a process requiring hundreds of thousands of technical adjustments and decisions during every launch flow. Nonetheless, it serves as a memorable example of a large organization learning, improving, and creating intangible human benefits.

The ebb and flow of business and technical improvements are complicated as well. Your teams, as Learning-Plus organizations, can similarly find the way to beef up the intangibles. It merely takes understanding and open-minded thinking.

The Ultimate Sophistication

Leonardo da Vinci, with arguably the most sophisticated human mind ever, noted, "Simplicity is the ultimate sophistication." We should never mistake a simplistic or sloppy approach to a problem for the kind of finessed, beautiful simplicity to which he referred. Da Vinci's simple sophistication is the refined and polished result of finding the optimum way of doing anything. It's safe to say that none of us has the genius to create a masterpiece like the *Mona Lisa*, but we can still apply this principle.

Push hard to know your business and technical matters so thoroughly that the creative, simple, "Why didn't I think of that?" solutions evolve. The more deeply prepared and aware your team is, the more elegantly simple your solutions will be. Along the way, you'll find more clarity and understanding in execution. It's a safe bet as well that your customers and users will find more value in your elegant work too. Operationally, simply effective execution can save valuable resources, particularly time.

In orbit during a human spaceflight, the most precious resource is crew time. The time crunch is particularly acute during the unbelievably busy and pressing timeframe of preparing to leave space and come home to the planet. During my first mission, I was one of two designated inflight maintenance (IFM) crewmembers for *Columbia*. The day before reentry, we discovered that the latches holding a large piece of research exercise equipment to the Spacelab floor had come loose. Subsequently, I received a rather disheartening six-page fax from MCC describing how to repair the intricate latch mechanisms.

It occurred to me that the real objective was to secure the equipment for reentry, not necessarily to fix the latches. A technician on Earth could repair the latches. No matter what, it would not do to have the device banging around during reentry maneuvers, potentially causing millions of dollars in damage. Within our give-and-take culture, I pushed back a bit with our control team.

"Houston, we've got some straps in the IFM kit. How about if I just lash down the ergometer nice and tight? It will save me an hour or so of time." A much simpler solution, and I really needed that time. The flight director agreed to the idea, so I tied my tightest Boy Scout diagonal lashings ever. That equipment wasn't going anyplace!

MCC had me video a "shake test" afterward for downlink and review to verify we were good to go. It passed muster. My old scoutmaster would've been proud. As I wrapped up, I also thought to snap a close-up photo of one of the lashings. I needed to show the kids in the troop for which I served as an assistant scoutmaster that we really can use lashings in the real world.

Sometimes even rocket science should not be rocket science! Innovation need not remain the exclusive domain of the "creatives" or product design types. Operational innovation, finding ways to get the job done better on the front line, is typically the product of 1,001 little "ahas" among line personnel, uncovered in the midst of straightforward problem solving. Simplicity rules.

Simple, elegant solutions are hallmarks of strong, execution-oriented teams. Powerfully aware teams surging into thoroughly planned, rehearsed, and communicated operations will enter a high-climbing results trajectory. Preparation and awareness are absolute musts. Teams continuing that climb with persistence and accountability will then also surely achieve complete success.

156 |

—CUE CARD—

DRIVE AWARENESS AND LEARNING

> **LEARN, STAY AWARE, CONSTANTLY IMPROVE FOR STRONGER PERFORMANCE AND PEAK COMPETENCE**

Result: Learning builds competence, while awareness protects and amplifies it.

Team Benefit: Continuous learning leads to increased confidence and satisfaction in expanded team capabilities.

Crew Notes for Business Execution:

8	Relentlessly promote discovery, curiosity, questioning, and learning.
7	A Learning-Plus team with a culture of expanding pertinent knowledge and practical skills adapts more quickly, operates with greater confidence, and can engage in more effective objective-oriented activity.
6	Mental simulations, rehearsals, and joint reviews of work scenarios provide a powerful supplement to formal training and book learning.
5	Strive for vigilant team situational awareness of the baseline and what may be "off-nominal." Always keep scanning.
4	Constantly iterate to improve. Team members should actively seek to make every aspect of team structure and action better.
3	Everyone, but particularly designated leaders, should humbly acknowledge their own mistakes while offering ideas to fix the shortcomings. Mistake-driven learning, if pursued with commitment to improve, is extremely effective in a team setting.
2	The larger the organization, the more difficult to build comprehensive mistake-trapping processes. Nevertheless, everyone should keep pushing such processes throughout the team and the broader organization.
1	Strive for elegant and simple—but not simplistic—solutions.

Spaceflight Metaphor: Continually improving is like an orbital rendezvous. It requires navigation (knowing where you are), guidance (seeing the path forward toward the target), and control (taking the right competency-enabled actions to get there).

PERSIST TO PREVAIL

"Success is often achieved by those who don't know that failure is inevitable."
—Coco Chanel

Purposeful Performance Principle 2: Leading all the way to successful completion requires tenacious persistence, acting in alignment with objectives, wisely mitigating risks, and patiently adjusting operations.

P
ersistence adds the will to overcome to the capability developed via preparation and awareness. Leaders need to demonstrate wise and patient persistence toward accomplishing mission objectives. If they build a robust culture of diligent, steady improvement, their team will overcome the most difficult obstacles.

Create the Future
In late 2003, six months after making my final move from government service, I was sitting quietly in my office working in my new role as an independent consultant and speaker. I had

served for a couple years in my post-astronaut career as a NASA research test pilot, flying the F-18 Hornet, F-15 Eagle, even the B-52, the exact same one from which we launched the X-15s and other exotic research aircraft back in the heyday of experimental flight test. While I had enjoyed flying those aircraft and working with some great people, NASA had cut way back on research project test flying. The focus had migrated from cutting-edge, risky research flight tests to other areas.

As much as I knew I would miss what flying I was getting, I concluded it was time to try something new, spring into action, and make a change. Almost immediately after taking the entrepreneurial plunge into business, I was able to begin connecting with other similar, action-oriented people in the private sector. Against this backdrop, I picked up the phone that autumn day.

"Hey, Rick, this is Peter. How's it going?" On the other end of the line was my friend Dr. Peter Diamandis. We'd worked together on one of my very first post-government consulting activities. I had helped him and the superb team at the Zero Gravity Corporation on the operations side as the company developed a private capability to fly parabolic zero-gravity flights for research and paying participants. I replied, "Just fine, Peter, knocking out some marketing materials."

Peter was already a legend among "space geeks" for his boldly imaginative ideas, irrepressibly persistent energy, and enthusiasm for all things space. Even as a Harvard Medical School MD, his true passion pulled him back to his undergraduate and master's field of aeronautics and astronautics. He had started several companies and space advocacy groups, each with a stunningly unique and imaginative focus. I had loved his active, energetic execution style with Zero G.

Of his many sayings, known as "Peter's Laws," my favorite one, which I took as a model for my own engagement in the imaginative "New Space" community, is this: "The best way to predict the future is to create it." Dr. Diamandis is now regarded as a foremost futurist and thought leader with the 2012 publication of his *New York Times* bestseller *Abundance: The Future Is Better than You Think.* Although his outlook has since significantly expanded to encompass virtually all fields, back then his focus was almost purely on space.

Continuing our conversation, Peter said, "Rick, you know about the X Prize, right, the other venture besides Zero G I've been working on?" Peter had founded the X Prize Foundation about five years earlier. "Of course, Peter, great stuff." Modeled on the Orteig Prize that Charles Lindbergh won back in 1927 for the first solo transatlantic flight, the Ansari X Prize was a ten million dollar prize to incentivize private space development, specifically for the first team to fly a reusable spacecraft to the edge of space. Winning the prize required attaining a minimum one hundred kilometers altitude, repeated within two weeks using the same vehicle, without government support or funding.

I was about to answer a question that would lead me to a much deeper understanding of this amazing project. Peter continued, "Well, we're looking for an independent and impartial chief judge to put a committee together to evaluate completion of all the requirements when one of our competing teams actually goes for it. Your astronaut experience would add great credibility. We know how much you enjoyed the team dynamics at Zero G. Plus, we have competitors registered from all over the world. You might get to travel to Australia, Europe, or Asia. Are you interested?"

"Well, yeah, absolutely, I'm in!" Over the next year, I worked closely with the X Prize Foundation and the company that eventually won the prize, Scaled Composites. I saw firsthand the active, results-producing execution resulting from a persistence that was the product of a deep commitment to a cause. We put together a dedicated, eclectic team to evaluate not only completion of technical benchmarks, but also the numerous other requirements. Serving as the Ansari X Prize chief judge gave me the privilege to announce the morning of October 4, 2004, in front of ten thousand future-leaning fans gathered at the Mojave Air & Space Port, a civilian flight test center in California, that we had a winner. Scaled Composites' Spaceship One had climbed to 112 kilometers altitude, nearly 368,000 feet high, breaking the forty-one-year-old X-15 absolute altitude record.

The winning of the Ansari X Prize provided a profound paradigm shift in how we would now envision human beings going to space. In the future, it would not just be the domain of massive government programs. The private sector could also begin to engage and create previously unconsidered capabilities. In the years since, many private entrepreneurial space technology companies have entered the fray. Initially, the community of space activists and fans, buoyed by the rush of the X Prize success, assumed that progress would happen virtually overnight. Many even believed that in just two or three years they'd be able to buy their own ticket to the edge of space.

Alas, reality in the space business is tough. Progress in this new segment of the aerospace industry has been steady, but not without difficulties, setbacks, and even fatalities. We're now many years past the time when the most starry-eyed optimists thought they'd go to space too. Nevertheless, many tenacious private companies, such as Space X (the first one to make it to orbit), Richard Branson's Virgin Galactic, and XCOR Aerospace, soldier on valiantly and patiently, building a new industry. Persistent dedication rules.

Pathways to Persistence

"Never give up. Never, ever give up." Short speech. Great man. Winston Churchill gave this speech to the US Congress right after World War II. He was a headstrong man who lived that maxim. With stubborn determination, he and his nation held on and persevered through the darkest hours. Therefore, all that persistence requires is stubborn determination, right? Not exactly. There is more.

Teams need to operate with an underlying tenacious mindset. Leaders must model firm resolution constantly. Everyone should strive to reinforce a steadfast staying power. How best to do that? By always keeping the desired end state in mind.

If you've paid careful attention to defining and internalizing your vision, purpose, and mission, the team will understand the ultimate destination. Those exercises weren't simply to fill a square or generate posters for the walls; mission statements exist to give the team the right focus during execution. The vision, purpose, and mission are the guiding stars. Furthermore, if you're concentrating on staying truly objective-centric, those objectives have created an entire suite of key waypoints.

What matters is that you reach the right objectives on the longer journey—not the exact, specific route you take to meet them. Alignment with objectives does not mean you'll always have an unobstructed beeline to them. If you start out on a given path but encounter insurmountable obstacles along the way, continuing to butt your head against the wall is counterproductive. Nonadaptive stubbornness is not effective persistence.

Flying into raging storms is no fun. Once, flying in a formation of aircraft not equipped with weather radar, my flight leader inadvertently dragged us into a powerful embedded thunderstorm. Instantly we went from soupy but smooth conditions to tooth-rattling severe turbulence. It was all I could do to stay on the wing and hope that he would quickly turn around. No such luck. He pressed on and hail shattered the optical nose cones of the four missiles hanging from the two aircraft. Ouch! Obstinate perseverance should've given way to finding another path toward the destination. You've got to know when to knock it off.

A fellow astronaut, Dr. Scott Parazynski, offers the best example I know of wisely knocking it off and persistently finding another pathway to the objective. An experienced mountaineer, Scott had always dreamed of summiting Mount Everest. In 2008 he intended to fulfill that dream, committing the time to train and the substantial money to join a climbing team for the May season. Many NASA colleagues also traveled to Nepal to support him from base camp at the foot of the Khumbu Icefall.

With repeated acclimatization trudges up to the various high camps and back, Scott was fit and ready to summit. However, on summit day at Camp IV, 26,300 feet above sea level on the Lhotse Face, an old back injury flared up, rendering his physical condition marginal to continue. With fulfillment of a lifelong dream in sight, imagine the alluring temptation to gut it out and go for it anyway. Scott wisely, and I'm sure with great heartache, decided that pressing on through the "death zone" would be foolish. He packed up and came down the mountain. That wisdom and moral courage impressed but did not surprise me. As soon as I learned what had happened, I fired off an email to Scott, one of congratulations for making the absolute right decision to back off when it really counted, under tremendous "go" pressure.

The dream remained, but the pathway changed. A disappointed astronaut climber came home, had back surgery, and decided to attempt the climb again the following year. Fully recovered, strong, and motivated, he summited at about four in the morning on May 20, 2009. I love the dawn photo of my beaming friend atop the highest point on the planet holding up a tiny piece of the moon NASA had lent him. Inspiration of the highest order!

For me, it was enough to peer down on Mount Everest from orbit while floating on the flight deck in shirtsleeve comfort, sipping on a drink. I figured I'd taken enough risks to get to that vantage point. Scott, to his great credit, is the only human to have peered down on Mount Everest from space and gazed up into space from Everest's summit. Were it not for his wisdom in corralling excess tenacity during the first attempt, it might not have turned out that way. The death zone is littered with bodies of climbers of lesser judgment. The objective-centric persistence of finding another way, patiently taking the long-range view instead of driving on with obdurate obsession on the path first chosen, makes the difference.

The MARS Route for Persistence during Execution

Persistence during execution consists primarily of getting and staying on track in alignment with the path to completing objectives. In our activities carrying out the program, we may get so busy that it's possible to suffer tunnel vision, even forgetting much of the preparation we've made and where we're supposed to be heading. The pressure's on; the clock is ticking, with no time to ponder! Four key attitudes and approaches will build the constantly correcting operations we need for success. Go to MARS in the heat of actual execution: **Mindset, Act Aligned, Risk Mitigate,** and **Steps** (yes, steps for the second time).

Mindset. Persistence takes energy and determination. The team needs to value an energetic pace to stay on top of challenges. The commander yet again sets the tone. The designated leader needs to show that progress and speed do matter. Waffling indecisiveness on his or her part puts a damper on execution that is very difficult for the rest of the team to overcome. Other team members should expand and grow that mindset while the leader acts as the leaven in the lump. Most pertinent for tenacious execution is the attitude that we must aggressively find and fix problems every day, with a real sense of urgency.

Many principles previously discussed come into play to reinforce this execution mindset: willingness to choose a difficult path, the ignition energy of passion, positively engaging in building trusting relationships, the confidence from continually rising competence, and many more. Though most were highlighted in other sections, all must coalesce and continue during operations. Coupling each of these multifaceted keys with a compelling sense of urgency unlocks the team's energies.

In his insightful book *The Acorn Principle*, my friend and noted business and sales expert Jim Cathcart perceptively counsels individuals to come to understand their own "optimum personal velocity." He explains the velocity concept, unsurprisingly, not as an engineer would, but as the self-development authority he is. For an individual, your personal velocity is the "combination of your energy patterns and your drive." He continues to highlight that an individual's personal velocity essentially reflects the intensity with which he or she approaches life. Of all the great concepts in this particular book, that one resonated with me the most.

In my family, I've been known since youth for my high intensity—whether for better or worse! I have a naturally high velocity. Although my wife maintains a more moderate and reasonable personal velocity, our oldest daughter, Megan, is also known for her intensity. No astronaut dream for her, though. From age three, she always wanted to be a ballet dancer. Her intense drive and focus led her to fulfill that dream; after college, she danced for six years as a professional with a top company, Ballet West, in Salt Lake City. It was just as exciting for our family to see her perform at the Kennedy Center for the Performing Arts in Washington, DC as it had been to witness my launches at the Kennedy Space Center. Megan and I achieved our goals largely due to intense personal velocity.

What's the relevance for teams? Should every single member of the team operate at an intensely high personal velocity? A resounding no! Team pace should be optimum, not breakneck. Speaking as a very high-velocity person, a homogenous team of all ultra-intense individuals would prove difficult to optimize and balance. The key within group and team activity is to point the individual velocities all in the same, aligned direction. Unlike Jim, I am an engineer, or more accurately now, a "recovering engineer." Velocity is to us engineers a vector quantity. In other words, it consists not just of the magnitude of speed, but a specific direction too. I believe, whether for individuals or teams, it's also useful to expand the human performance velocity concept to that vector, combining magnitude and direction.

Persistent leaders and teams cultivate the right sense of urgency and eagerness for progress. Doing so will produce a proactive mindset. That's the magnitude. Then leaders need to point the group in the right direction. That makes it a vector. Attitude, contrary to what some may say, is certainly not everything, but in the midst of execution, it will direct you and the team where you need to go. An axiom from instrument flying is "attitude determines altitude." How you set your orientation, or pitch angle, coupled with airplane performance from speed and throttle setting, will determine where in the sky the airplane ends up. It's the exact same way with our teams. With the right team mindset of optimum speed and correct, objective-pointed direction, we can act in alignment with our purpose and plans.

Act Aligned. With a cohesive team and the right initial velocity vector, you're headed off the launch pad perfectly. All's well. Nothing will upset the flight, and you'll stay on track, right? If only it were that easy! The team has to constantly work at rapidly fixing issues and shortfalls that inevitably will arise. Acting aligned is the balancing of every element within execution to stay pointed toward objectives at the center of the PAPA orbital system. It requires patiently staying on top of the work, as closely as possible. Tracking that alignment and guiding realignment are fundamental executive leadership skills.

It's now time to consider just how to steer a rocket. You probably won't ride one anytime soon, but that steering process is exactly like keeping all those balls in the air in the execution juggling that you do have to do. The concept is very simple, even though the implementation is not. On the space shuttle, all the rocket engine nozzles can tilt in various directions. Through the apparent magic of some elegant software, guidance and control sensors, and very heavy-duty hydraulics, the system automatically moves those massive nozzles, or gimbals them (to use the rocket science term). The rapid, precise adjustments continually keep nudging the rocket back to its planned flight path.

On board in flight, you really don't feel those continual small adjustments. The net result is that the launching space shuttle appears to scoot along as if on rails. All the while, however, the sensors, computers, and aft-end hardware

are working nonstop, continually closing the loop and aligning the actual flight path with the desired trajectory. In execution, we need to work equally as hard in following our own guidance to our targets. It's never-ending, adjusting what we do to stay pointed toward our objectives.

Risk Mitigate, Real Time. Hopefully in the preparation phases you've carefully, with a disciplined process, evaluated all the risks to your operation your team could possibly envision. Nevertheless, in the real world, unknown risks still lurk. You must expect the unexpected. This process also needs to happen constantly. Buoyed with strong situational awareness, the team will anticipate and quickly perceive when new risks arise or old ones flare up with more potency.

A powerful tactic in real-time risk analysis is to build into your crosscheck "downside sensitivity." Even while staying optimistic about what you're doing, force a subroutine to run in everyone's minds that queries what might go wrong at any point. Then ask yourselves what the initial and follow-on responses should be. This skill is actually another facet of situational awareness. The sensitivity to when the baseline is starting to tilt in a negative way gives you the heads-up that it's all starting to go south.

In any flight operation, this downside sensitivity skill is valuable. It's sometimes said that aviation consists of "hours of boredom interrupted by sheer terror." While I don't totally agree with that characterization, the ability to anticipate, risk mitigate, and minimize the impact of the anxiety-filled moments can prove very useful.

One of the very rewarding contract professional flying activities I do regularly now is with the flight test company Flight Research, Inc. Our team has developed an intense, three-day course flying Sabreliner business jets and Impalas (military-origin, single-engine, advanced jet trainers), at the very edges of their flight envelopes. Like the team's other very experienced jet instructors and test pilots, I take commercial business jet pilots far out of their normal comfort zone for the sake of training. With full FAA approval, we train them on how to deal with aircraft stalls, unusual pitch and roll attitudes, and major flight path upsets, any one of which could really ruin their day if it happened inadvertently during line operations. Mighty fun for a guy who's now a grandpa to go hop in an ejection-seat-equipped jet and fly it to the limit!

Even more gratifying as an advanced jet flight instructor is to see the growth in situational awareness and downside sensitivity we're able to develop in these professional pilots. These pilots are all very skilled in their operational realm but just haven't had the chance to do much of this type of flying. They certainly would never do it intentionally with passengers on board. However, even we instructor pilots, with our deep experience conducting flight tests and flying and spinning aircraft at the edges of the envelope, have to constantly stay ahead of the jets and our business aviation client pilots. When you're upside down in an inverted spin, eyeballs bugging out from the negative G and the windscreen filled with desert whipping around below you as the altimeter winds down, it helps to be ready for anything. Real-time, dynamic, execution-risk mitigation makes you ready.

While your particular operations are likely not quite so physically demanding, business team activities these days are no less dynamic in terms of the number of changes, new issues arising, and risks rearing their ugly heads. While executing, you must stay ready to adjust to the negatives that inevitably appear without letting them drag you down. Maintain the proactive risk mitigation posture, keep the situational awareness up, and exercise downside sensitivity, even while energetically pressing forward.

Steps, Again. The least dramatic of execution persistence skills, this phase begins with constantly comparing the process steps you're taking with what you had planned. Verify alignment with the steps you've developed in the planning process and then fully brief everyone. Change those steps as necessary. Your plan may be awesome, but it still needs to evolve real time. Helmuth von Moltke, a Prussian field marshal in the mid-nineteenth century, counseled, "No plan survives first contact with the enemy." Your enemy is the real-world business environment, as changeable and unforgiving as it is.

Human space operations dedicate an entire eight-hour shift daily, the "planning shift," to update and replan crew activities based on the feedback and results of the previous day. Crew and controllers then need to jointly flex to implement the new and improved plan. Ideally, most of those plan changes are proactive improvements. However, some changes are necessary reactions to malfunctions and problems. The following anecdote exemplifies this process, but also highlights that leaders can't shy away from getting their hands dirty either, sometimes literally.

Somewhat to our chagrin, *Columbia*'s toilet broke in space during my command mission, STS-90. Actually, the problem was not particularly severe. Underneath the toilet itself, in the plumbing that NASA politely called the wastewater lines, we had developed a blockage. The good news was that with redundant plumbing lines, even the space toilet had multiple backups. It would be a pretty simple fix. The bad news was that when Mission Control had set the time when we would fix it, my other IFM crewmate, copilot Scott Altman, was right in the middle of supporting an important payload activity. I momentarily slightly regretted my preflight encouragement for him to take the deep dive into Neurolab science, for I would've gladly delegated to Scott this particular task!

Pulling out the necessary tools and the procedure, I took my own deep dive underneath *Columbia*'s space toilet. Not yet too put off, I always thought it quite fun to turn wrenches on a multibillion dollar spaceship while zipping along at five miles a second. Everything started well. The procedure was straightforward. The closeout panels came off nicely, so I had ready access to everything. I have fairly small hands, so there was no problem getting the tools in where I needed them. No particular odor either. No worries.

Then I disconnected the line, exactly in accordance with the procedure. The slight overpressure started pushing out a globule of yellowish liquid, primarily urine only slightly diluted by water from the onboard humidity separators. Yaa! It quickly grew to the size of a grapefruit, drifting lazily in all its glory right in front of my face. The distinct thought came to mind, *This whole astronaut job isn't nearly as glamorous as everyone thinks!* There was nothing else to do but grab a towel and sop it up, getting my hands thoroughly soaked too. Then I quickly rerouted the line to the alternate fitting and finished the task. Finally, I scrubbed and scrubbed, though a faint trace of the odor lingered on my hands for over a day. Oh well, the things we do to fly in space.

Fixing *Columbia*'s plumbing was one of many hundreds of Step process adjustments in the execution of a very complex human spaceflight. This particular evolution was typical for how we adapted and persisted in the face of problems big or small. I must admit, though, floating in close formation with yesterday's juices and hot drinks made for a spaceflight memory that I will never forget—even if it is not my most treasured.

Active, real-time team execution is, for the high-intensity person like myself, the best work of all. Nothing beats being where the action is. The exertion, no matter how strenuous, is fun, invigorating, and high impact. However, such activity can only really be worthwhile when it accomplishes objectives for meaningful results that support the ultimate purpose. Accordingly, you must persistently and repeatedly realign actions with objectives and tactical execution with the overall strategy.

You have to slog through all the details from start to finish for complete success. The thirty-nine days total I've spent in space only came to fruition after many years of preparation and represent just the tip of the iceberg of the many and varied team activities of which I've been a part through the years. Team endeavors in human spaceflight encompass far more than just the inflight portion, or even specific flight training, covering every aspect of a supremely difficult undertaking. It takes plain-old hard work and determined tenacity in preparation and action. Most of it is not glamorous, whether or not it's as unglamorous as toilet repairs.

Regardless of the venture, industry, or team specifics, the same guidance applies. To get to the point of springing off the launch pad and accelerating into action, you and your successful team will have paid a lot of dues. Relish those efforts. Embrace all phases and principles; work them hard. Persist regardless of the obstacles. Then you can watch your team come together to produce the kind of sterling results such efforts deserve!

—CUE CARD—

PERSIST TO PREVAIL

> ### TENACIOUSLY EXERCISE
> ### OBJECTIVE-ALIGNED PERSISTENCE

Result: Objective-aligned persistence empowers execution all the way through completion without falling short.

Team Benefit: Tenacious leaders strengthen team will and attitude of ownership.

Crew Notes for Business Execution:

9	Preparation and awareness provide the capability, and persistence gives the will to execute all the way to successful completion.
8	Stubborn determination and never giving up is most, but not all, that persistence requires.
7	Always keep the desired end state in mind so that, if necessary, you can adjust the path and the waypoint objectives to get there.
6	A four-part format, MARS, for Mindset, Adjust to Act Aligned, Risk Mitigate, and Steps, will guide actions to reinforce persistent, corrective progress.
5	Mindset requires leaders decisively demonstrate a sense of urgency to fix issues while all team members support and grow that attitude.
4	An effective team velocity vector consists of the optimum magnitude of unified willpower headed in a continually realigned direction.
3	Acting aligned requires constant, rapid, and precise adjustments to stay close to our desired course toward objectives.
2	Expect the unexpected to mitigate risks real time. Cultivate "downside sensitivity," an important component of situational awareness.
1	Constantly compare execution steps and workflow with those planned and briefed. Continually refine, replan, and adjust the process steps as needed.

Spaceflight Metaphor: Steering a rocket through tilting its engines keeps the flight path aligned with the desired trajectory. The constant and precise corrections model the persistent alignment concepts teams should use during execution.

PROPEL ACCOUNTABILITY
FOR RESULTS

"I pass with relief from the tossing sea of Cause and Theory to the firm ground of Result and Fact."
—**Winston Churchill**

Purposeful Performance Principle 1: Execution excellence demands total accountability, principled adaptability, and a disciplined debriefing mindset.

Operations in dynamic environments dictate immediate, accountable responses to fix mistakes and keep progressing toward meeting objectives. Leaders should build a team ethos of voluntary, no-excuse accountability for all results. Such an accountability climate closes the loop in the PAPA system to keep moving the team to crisper execution. It requires principled adaptability, or changing as

aligned with values and objectives, versus mushy, undirected flexibility. Finally, a disciplined execution communication and debriefing mindset powerfully promotes an accountability culture.

Staying Alive at Mach 18

It was close to midnight. I was exhausted after a sixteen-hour day that had wrapped up with a four-hour simulator session. I needed to vent just a little. "Hey, Chili, that sim went great. We're way up on the step. Can't we get the training team to back off just a little?" With an all-veteran crew and months to go until launch, we were well ahead, practically ready to fly right then.

Kevin Chilton, our wise commander, answered, "No, sorry, but we're going to take every single chance we can to keep getting better." His principled response was the product of his deep sense of accountability as commander to make certain his crew was absolutely ready for every possible contingency on launch day. Nodding, I replied, "I know, I know. Let me get some sleep and I'll be ready to hit it hard again tomorrow."

In the last few months before a launch, an astronaut crew lives and breathes virtually nothing except the upcoming mission. One-hundred-plus-hour work weeks are not uncommon and the pace is brutal. The PAPA elements of preparation and persistence predominate because of the supreme need to raise our awareness and skills to the very high standards to which we are held accountable.

Fast forward three months to 3:20 a.m. on March 17, 1996, about 150 miles abeam North Carolina, 360,000 feet high. We're headed northeast in *Atlantis* at over 12,000 miles per hour, approaching eighteen times the speed of sound. I'm a happy rocket man. The three main engines, my systems since I'm in the right seat, purr along splendidly. We're just about to throttle back so we don't exceed 3 "Gs" of acceleration. Sure, we all weigh nearly three times normal, but the seats are well padded, and there's no need to get up and run around. Pretty nice ride, as long as you don't think too much about how you might die doing it. Everything's great—until instantly it isn't!

Suddenly the annoyingly loud warning alarm bleats out and our systems display starts blinking its "HYD PRESS LOW" message. A fraction of a second later our ascent CAPCOM, another pilot astronaut in Mission Control, calls,

"*Atlantis*, we show a system-three hydraulic leak. P-L-T, execute Hydraulic Leak procedure." I verify the onboard data. Sure enough, hydraulic fluid is draining like an open spillway at Hoover Dam. Confirming with Chili, I say, "I show system three." He concurs. It's over to the hydraulics panel by my right knee.

Wearing bulky multilayer pressure suit gloves, I gingerly reach for the correct switch. Lined up in a row, each of the three hydraulic system isolation switches is only about an inch apart. Big glove or not, better grab the correct one, and only one. If I shut down the wrong system, we all die. The "power steering" for *Atlantis*—hydraulically driven engine bells—works fine with two systems, but not with just one. With fluid lost in one system, an incorrect isolation of either remaining system means game over. Corkscrewing through the sky while out of control at twenty times the speed of sound is not how I want to end my day—or my life. After that most critical first step, I quickly complete the rest of the procedure.

Though potentially just an inch away from dying, we were in reality a long way from that outcome. I had performed that same procedure hundreds of times in high-fidelity simulators, even wearing the exact same type gloves. It was so ingrained in my mind that I could've done it in my sleep. In fact, occasionally during the intense training, I dreamed of handling various emergencies. Pretty effective use of time to train in your dreams! I don't think my heart rate even increased while executing what I'd been so prepared to do. In the heat of that battle, I felt acutely aware of every single thing going on. The preparation had given me vigilant situational awareness, but that preparation had required the persistence to "keep getting better" in those many long, often late-night simulations.

After we reached main engine cutoff (MECO) a minute later it really struck me what had just transpired. Now weightless, the hydraulic problem handled correctly, and the adrenaline jolt over, my nerves felt free to jangle a bit. My heart rate did go up then as I pondered that this time it was no simulation. I truly was accountable to my crewmates, their families, NASA, and the American taxpayer. I said a short prayer of thanks that I had come through and taken good care of *Atlantis* when she started "bleeding." We could all thank an obsessively persistent training philosophy and a commander relentlessly leading his team to operational excellence. I was grateful too for living and working in a team culture of personal accountability that spurred each of us on to our absolute best.

Had I executed incorrectly, the STS-76 crew and I would not be alive today, nor would *Atlantis* now be on display at Kennedy Space Center. We would've all ended up at the bottom of the Atlantic Ocean. Instead, we completed a full mission and returned home safely to our families. Chances are you've never heard of this situation, one of the more serious ascent emergencies ever in the Space Shuttle Program. That's fine, and it's a great tribute to NASA's robust crew-training system that we made it look like a nonevent. The successful resolution of this operational challenge required absolutely perfect execution. It highlights every element of the PAPA Effective Execution System: Preparation, Awareness, Persistence, and Accountability, all applied with real urgency toward a focused objective. In this case the objective was a dramatically compelling one: staying alive and preserving a multibillion-dollar national asset.

Anyone, to perform at the very highest level, must resolutely hold themselves accountable for results and continuous improvement. Trials and difficulties are inevitable. Emergencies, or as NASA euphemistically calls them, "off-nominal situations," happen. True leaders always set the example of how to deal with such challenges. They build awareness and capability through preparation, exercise their willpower in persistence, and model a dedication to accountability. That accountability ethos consolidates effective execution and advances the team to the next level. Then leaders and the team begin another orbit around the PAPA system while continuing to focus attention on the objectives below.

Real-Time Accountability

The dynamic world of military aviation and the astronaut business impose instant accountability. Conditions can go from normal to disastrous instantaneously. If you fall short, the first indication may be a fireball from a midair collision or smacking into a mountain. This reality requires an attitude of constantly trapping errors and holding each other strictly accountable, as quickly as possible. The environment dictates a culture of real-time accountability. The linchpin of such a culture is the willingness to accept critiques and take immediate action to fix problems.

Within any team, multiple levels of group and individual accountability exist. Laws, ethical standards, and regulatory impositions make us answerable on one level. Company policies determine another set of standards. If we assume that a given team understands and complies with all the externally imposed requirements, what's left? The two main areas of near real-time accountability are shared group accountability and individuals answering to each other for their own work.

The first, shared team accountability, relates to overall results and the organization itself. A truly high-performing team will incorporate systems to ensure a given work package, project, or operation gets done. With clarity and decisiveness, such a team will assess objective accomplishment and fix the shortfalls. To best do so, the team itself has to have authority to define most of the parameters of its structure, organization, and workflow. Beyond general "what" guidelines, the "how" details should be left to the team itself. Leaders should not generally prescribe detailed methods, but should focus on desired results.

In practice, shared team accountability is potentially problematic. If everyone is responsible, then maybe no one can really be held responsible. Remember the belly button? It's a conundrum without an easy answer. An effective way to avoid this trap is to consider shared team accountability as the multiple of inter-team trust times the sum of individual team members' buy-in to personal accountability. Accordingly, keep focusing on expanding trust while also building the nodes of people who step up and answer for their performance. Much like individual trustworthiness prefaces the first-order team trust requirement, stand-up people willing to take action and accept consequences build a shared group accountability culture.

Many previously discussed principles contribute to people standing up as highly accountable individuals. Trust, removing fear of punishment for honest mistakes, transparent standards and leaders, and a service-to-others outlook all help. The ideal team member will comfortably operate within a trusting framework to instantly accept and act upon valid constructive criticism. Furthermore, everyone will tactfully but frankly offer those critiques to others for the good of the team.

In the perfect shared-accountability team, no offense is ever intended, none ever taken, and all is for the good of mission accomplishment. Accountability culture is a powerful multiplier. Another related accountability enhancer is to always follow through.

Follow Through with Accountability: 98 Percent Doesn't Hack It

During space shuttle launches, the external fuel tank remained attached all the way to space. Eighteen seconds after main engine cutoff, we'd hear a massive "clunk" as the pyrotechnic charges fired and the tank separated. Orbiter, crew, and tank were all in space but still a few hundred miles per hour less than the 17,500 miles per hour to stay in orbit. With over 98 percent of the speed needed to stay in orbit, the separated external tank would still begin to descend, at first slowly, then with increasing rapidity. We could watch it passing over the clouds below as it tumbled end over end into the atmosphere, eventually fragmenting and mostly burning up. A few of the larger chunks would survive the fiery fall to plunge into the ocean. In contrast, by firing the smaller orbital maneuvering system engines for just a couple minutes more, metaphorically persisting with that final little nudge, the orbiter and crew reached the objective of staying in orbit.

The space shuttle system was designed to operate that way, but how often do teams or individuals fizzle out just short of their objectives? That last bit of effort often makes all the difference. Falling short reflects a deficit in follow-through, a major component of accountability for results. Check, recheck, validate, trust but verify, and follow up with all your people, all the time. Don't assume you're there until past the finish line, still striding strong the whole way. The leader's role, with ideally every team member supporting, is to model how to be a finisher. Close the loop with accountability for results.

Principled Adaptability Trumps Indecisive Flexibility

People typically equate adaptability with flexibility. In Objective-Centric Execution, however, an important distinction exists. Adaptability is longer term and requires holding oneself and the team responsible for making positive, productive changes. Accordingly, adaptability is directly tied to accountability.

Adaptability must align in integrity with objectives and the organization's values to produce principled adaptability.

Short-term flexibility can have value, but may also just be mushy and nonproductive. Think of a reed blowing any which way in the wind. It never, metaphorically, stands up for anything. Flexibility, as it describes mental agility and quickness, has significant execution value. As it might describe indecision and waffling, it's frustrating at best, debilitating often. Indecisive, inappropriately flexible leaders hold back real execution.

Today's business environment requires high speed execution. We must take advantage of just-in-time supply chains, drive down product development times, and instantly respond to customers. More than just a competitive advantage, speed is a survival requirement. As important as execution speed is, a more important factor is agility. Nimble leaders and teams that can quickly change direction are more flexible responding to short-term needs and, over the long run, more adaptable. Agility is also a very important component of accountable execution. Those operating in a results-oriented accountability culture more quickly identify when a given course of action isn't really taking the team directly toward its objectives. Then they can adroitly make the necessary changes needed to get back on track.

The difference between a hard-charging yet unadaptable team and a highly agile team is like comparing a returning space shuttle to a fighter aircraft. On reentry at fifteen times the speed of sound, a reentering orbiter has a turn radius of several states! Though hypersonic in speed, it's not agile at all. An F-18, much slower but pulling many Gs, almost turns inside of itself. Quick, responsive flight path changes are the mark of the nimble, adaptable team as well.

Celebrate All Along the PAPA Orbit

Accountability and all the other requirements for strong execution are serious subjects. Nevertheless, during the intensity of daily operations, it's also helpful for leaders to hold themselves accountable for the intangibles of team spirit and inspiration. In addition to the numerous matrix-building and balance-generating techniques previously discussed, you should also consider the following ideas.

Leaders, you need to exude confidence—even if you don't entirely feel it yourself. It's contagious. Encouragement and simple, positive affirmations within the team are powerful endurance enhancers. Nothing entirely replaces regular face-to-face contact in promoting these encouraging interactions. Reminders of past positive results reenergize us. Leaders should leverage previous successes in pulling the team toward current objectives.

It helps to pull the nose off the grindstone on occasion and reinvigorate ourselves. Take a breather as needed. Climbing the mountains toward the team's objectives, we should also positively reaffirm progress by regularly looking back at the valley floor to see how far we've come. Celebrate the small wins.

A space shuttle launch provides an interesting analogue to this principle. Going "uphill" from a standing start to 17,500 miles per hour takes only eight and a half minutes but is chock full of accountable performance milestones, all based on velocity. As each one is ticked off, the crew and the team in MCC mentally celebrate a small win. With each event, you're closer to being safely in orbit.

As we gain more velocity during ascent, these benchmarks pass, all related to our status in case of a main engine failure: "Two engine Zaragoza." OK, on two engines we can cover the remaining distance across the Atlantic to an emergency landing site in Spain. "Press to ATO" (Abort to Orbit). An assist from the OMS engines will get us to a low but safe orbit. "Press to MECO." Even with a subsequent engine failure, we'll make it to orbit for a full mission. That's a sweet call to hear!

To celebrate the small wins, cultivate a fun-seeking attitude. As commander, the first thing I said to the STS-90 crew at the start of our long, uphill training climb was, "If we're not having fun, we're doing something wrong!" The climb ahead should always be challenging, demanding, even exhausting—but never unenjoyable, burdensome, or miserable.

We have hundreds of metrics in business to measure the results for which we are accountable, in virtually every area imaginable. Do we have an internal metric for gauging the fun level—not purposeless, idle amusement, but the gratifying fun of steady progress with our team? Such a qualitative gauge will help the leader know when to push extra hard or back off just a bit in leading the team around their PAPA orbit as they execute.

Just like any project needs pertinent milestones, so too should the team intuitively grasp when fun milestones are needed. Hold yourselves accountable to them. Intentionally celebrate, take a break, and congratulate one another as you make progress! The effective team will not groan constantly under the load, but resolutely and energetically march forward, enjoying the journey. The leader should stay one step ahead on that journey to reach back and help pull the team along.

Communications for Accountable Execution

A significant aspect of every PAPA category is reflected in how teams communicate under the pressure of ongoing action. In addition to various communications and briefing keys outlined previously, active execution communications bear a bit more discussion. These real-time team interactions support alignment with objectives and typically provide the ongoing feedback to measure accountability for results. Pulling on the vector concept again, magnitude and unified direction matter for internal and external communications.

First, internally, it is virtually impossible to over-communicate the elements of vision, purpose, mission, and especially goals and objectives to the team, even while everyone is cranking out the work. Regular promptings are helpful. Written reminders, clearly visible, make a lot of sense. For each of the various teams and partnerships with which I stay involved, I keep a short "cue card" handy to remind me regularly of what we're really all about.

Most important in aligning execution communications with the strategic stuff is to stay focused on the objectives in the center of your orbit. This alignment requires regular crosschecks. Whether formally or informally, everyone needs to keep assessing and freely sharing their evaluations of how the team is doing with respect to those objectives. That is the essence of a real-time accountability culture. You're gimbaling those rocket engines, remember, and it is a nonstop undertaking. Inherent to the process, like the electrical signals between sensors, computers, and on-engine control units, is nonstop communication.

Team communication during execution with external customers or stakeholders absolutely requires alignment with team purpose and objectives. Teams need to carefully craft unified messages, whether formal or informal. The team should even consider and shepherd the subtle nonverbal and unwritten signals it puts out to make sure those indications are consistent with objectives. Every organization should speak in unison. At best, divergent crosstalk coming out of the team confuses other members of your matrix to the nth power. At worst, if intentionally done for selfish or thoughtless reasons, it will chip away at the team and vastly diminish positive impact external to the group.

When I first arrived in Houston for astronaut training, I found the organizational communication dynamics between the Astronaut Office and the many other important Johnson Space Center divisions fascinating yet sometimes puzzling. At the time, we had about seventy active astronauts, including a few folks from Apollo days and most of the original 1978 and subsequent space shuttle classes. Furthermore, many senior engineers and operational support people had been there since the early days of the space program. As a brand-new guy in my first year, I stayed almost exclusively in receive mode. Later, after my initial training, I often communicated externally on behalf of the astronaut office while serving in various technical assignments.

Coming as I did from the Air Force, I was used to clear chains of command and lines of communication. Traditional military units are, as one would expect, quite hierarchal. NASA, by contrast and design, operated with a flatter, less formal organization. Multiple communications pathways and opportunities to pursue your division's agenda existed. One very interesting communications situation—a holdover, I believe, from earlier days in the program when we had far fewer astronauts—occurred fairly regularly. I didn't think it was optimum.

The interaction typically played out as follows: You, an engineer or ops person, need crew office buy-in on a particular change or initiative. OK, head over to Building 4 South, wander through the Astronaut Office on the top floor until finding someone, anyone, then try to convince him of your position and get a sign-off. By the way, finding an astronaut hanging out in the office is never a sure thing, with all the external duties, time in simulators, flying, traveling, and so forth. The result is that pretty much one astronaut's signature is as good as another's. Once the change form is signed, you're good to go!

Often that informal process worked just fine. Just as often, though, it could lead to challenges and dilute real accountability. If, for whatever technical reasons, the actual designated crew office representative disagreed with the position of the other organization, it was rife with potential miscues. Regardless, it was not the optimum communications approach for the Astronaut Office to take. Under the leadership of Chief Astronaut Colonel Bob Cabana, I witnessed significant improvement in our external communications effectiveness. Bob insisted that, regardless of how minor the issue was, the crew office would speak with a unified voice. We would take the little extra time to coordinate internally and present one Astronaut Office opinion. In short order, this improved process injected a tighter discipline into our own reviews and gave greater communications clarity across the larger organization. We acted with more alignment, the communications vector pointing in the right direction. Accordingly, the chain of accountability became stronger and the overall effectiveness within the larger organization improved.

The Debriefing Culture

Debriefing well gives a powerful boost to accountable, results-driven execution. In my leadership consulting and speaking the last ten years, I've rarely seen business clients use any type of dedicated debriefing, at least until I can convince them of its tremendous value. I believe because time is money and we're always in a hurry to rush into the next activity, we neglect to close that loop. However, debriefing benefits amply justify the time invested. Timely, in-person debriefings will enhance team performance.

The flight's not over until after the debriefing. Every Air Force sortie I flew concluded with a no-holds-barred, lessons-extracting, formal debriefing. For a two-week space shuttle mission, the multiple sessions would run for an additional two weeks, eight to ten hours a day. Rarely are debriefings that extensive. In fact, depending on the activity, a useful one may need to last just a few minutes.

Prior to landing *Columbia*, I had performed, like all commanders, over twelve hundred practice shuttle landing approaches, typically ten per sortie. We flew those flights in NASA's Shuttle Training Aircraft, a modified Gulfstream II business jet. Due to some very clever modifications, it handled and performed exactly like the orbiter during approach and landing. After each approach, while climbing out and setting up for the next one, I pored over a detailed printout with every performance parameter imaginable: touchdown speed and location, sink rate, pitch angle, controller inputs, and many more. I quickly debriefed the approach with the STA safety pilot—an experienced NASA research pilot—then flew another one. The sum of those quick debriefings over the years provided the myriad of subtle perceptual, mental, and hand-eye coordination improvements I would need to bring home a two billion dollar winged orbiter with only one chance. When I grabbed hold of *Columbia*'s stick during reentry after sixteen days in space, it felt exactly like the STA. I knew I was ready.

Simply put, debriefing makes you better, often with nearly as much impact as practicing the operation itself.

The main reasons to hold debriefings are to capture learning, share best practices, promote accountability, and invigorate execution follow-through. A logical debriefing structure helps capture the most benefits from the time spent. Accordingly, here is a framework—one last acronym—that we've found extremely useful. Remember to come back down to EARTH for well-grounded, productive debriefings: **Execution, Accountability, Review, Timeline (and Timely),** and **Highlight.**

Execution. The "what." Compare what actually transpired to the objective. Objective-centric, remember? With every orbit around the PAPA Effective Execution System, we focus on what we're trying to accomplish. This step is the big picture. If you fell short of any objectives, you need to get that out on the table right away. No use tiptoeing around the elephant in the room. Alternately, you may have met the objective, but if the execution was painfully sloppy, there's still plenty of room for improvement. Or the team may have nailed it with aplomb. Time to celebrate, but still look for opportunities to execute better. You can always improve.

Accountability. The "why and who." The key in frank discussions of accountability is to start with considering the systemic or organizational whys of any shortcomings. Keep it data driven and fact intensive. Think systems and processes. With that joint analysis complete, and in a serious but cooperative spirit, then press the belly buttons. In a high-performing, shared accountability team, people will immediately self-identify if they've come up short. Then they'll also offer ideas for improvement. Wrap up accountability discussions with assigning one or more individuals further responsibility to fix specific issues.

Few examples are stronger than when a leader also accepts any deserved blame contritely and commits publicly to do better. As a young Air Force captain, I witnessed a very senior leader model this principle while debriefing during a huge Red Flag exercise at Nellis Air Force Base, Nevada, that involved hundreds of people and billions of dollars of aircraft and other assets. The "air war" that day had not gone well at all. Very few of us attackers made it through unscathed to our targets. This high-ranking officer, who had led the strike package, humbly took full blame and proceeded to teach us how he would correct the situation and what we all needed to do to execute better. We adjusted our tactics the next day with greatly improved results. Though I've long forgotten the details of that exercise, I'll never forget the deep respect and appreciation I gained for this outstanding role model.

Review. The "how." Review process and procedure details. If you're in a truly empowered team, you will have large latitude in determining just how you get the work done. From a viewpoint of shared accountability to your stakeholders, pay attention to improving process. Optimizing future performance relies on full understanding, discussion, and improvement of process details.

Timeline (and Timely). The "when." Go over the time dimension of the entire execution package you're debriefing. Time's always a valuable resource. Was any wasted? Did you deliver on time? What were the delays and their causes? How might you streamline the process in the future?

You should hold the debriefing as quickly as possible while the activities are still fresh in everyone's mind. It helps too, as with any meeting, to start and end on time. If it becomes obvious that you will go over, either get unanimous team buy-in or schedule another session.

Highlight. Summarize the key lessons learned. Identify where the written record will reside for everyone's reference. Quickly review a few lows of the operation and the plan going forward to fix them. End on a high note with the top two or three best ideas or practices. Walk out the door squared away and happy to be members of a focused, effective team.

Debriefing diligently, embracing accountability, adapting, persisting in light of the desired end, and exercising steadfast determination are all directly related. Each is a crucial active execution skill. Together these actions toughen any team. Latched on to preparation and awareness, persistence and accountability surround and point toward the central, objective-based core of the PAPA system for capable team execution.

184 |

— CUE CARD —

PROPEL ACCOUNTABILITY FOR RESULTS

> **HOLD SELF AND TEAM ACCOUNTABLE**
> **FOR USEFUL, REAL RESULTS**

Result: Accountability closes the loop of all execution activities to ensure the team meets objectives.

Team Benefit: Team members earn the gratification and tangible benefits that come from executing all the way to mission success.

Crew Notes for Business Execution:

8	A real-time, honest, shared-accountability culture, where all team members willingly stand up and eagerly accept responsibility, is a powerful multiplier of team efforts.
7	Be a finisher! Check, recheck, validate, trust but verify, and follow up with all your people, all the time, to close the accountability loop.
6	Principled adaptability, accountable to objectives and values, spurs wise changes. It trumps waffling, indecisive flexibility every time.
5	Leaders, hold yourself accountable to cultivate informal "fun metrics" to celebrate the progress and small wins along the way and thus reward and inspire your team.
4	It's virtually impossible to over-communicate aspects of vision, purpose, mission, and especially objectives to the team, even while everyone is cranking out the work.
3	Effective communications provide the ongoing feedback to measure accountability for results and drive unity of action.
2	Investing the time and effort to conduct formal debriefings will make you better and may have nearly as much positive impact on long-term execution success as the operation itself.
1	The down-to-EARTH debriefing covers Execution (what), Accountability (why and who), Review of the operation (how), Timeline (when), and Highlights.

Spaceflight Example: Surviving the only space shuttle ascent hydraulic failure required the will to prepare persistently and acceptance of accountability for the lives of others, resulting in the necessary level of high-awareness for perfect execution.

LIFTOFF TO SUCCESS

"The beginnings and endings of all human undertakings are untidy."
—**John Galsworthy**

P urposeful Performance Principles within Purpose, People, Perspective, and Program converge not just to build a team, but also to yield productive, mission-accomplishing real work from the team. Effective execution follows from focusing on objectives at the right pace while employing principles of Preparation, Awareness, Persistence, and Accountability.

Clear of the Pad

The countdown is over and the initial jolt of the engines lighting has kicked you off the pad. You're the in-flight leader, accelerating as you never have before.

Your team is heading upward on that trajectory, or flight path, that will either deposit you safely at your targets or see you go down in flames. It's up to you. Time for you and your team to perform!

The 4P model of Purpose, People, Perspective, and Program defines an arc of growth, work, and accomplishment for any team. These four broad categories cover all aspects from initial team formation, getting to know and appreciate one another, establishing direction and standards, seeing the potential, and acting energetically to fulfill the team's mission. Within the 4P arc, certain specific Purposeful Performance Principles fit nicely within each category. One finds tremendous overlap between all elements. All must contribute in a balanced fashion to proceed successfully from first establishing a given team all the way through to the team truly fulfilling its purpose with tangible, stellar results.

We've considered the principles during the countdown just before springing off the launch pad. Now, as you embark on your own team-powered flight, let's briefly review the key aspects of the countdown within the overarching flow of the four Ps. The principles are timeless, tested, and true. Employing them will empower your team to enjoy a successful ascent.

Purpose: The Why

At the very outset of the team lifetime, leaders and team members must consider first things first. To establish the type of team that will powerfully get things done, the team must ask of itself guiding star questions: "What is our desired end state? What is our overriding, highest priority purpose? What mission will fulfilling that purpose serve?"

Right at the start, a Choose the Hard mentality informs that entire questioning process. The best end state takes the most devotion. Such commitment emboldens the team, inspires individual members, and makes everything that follows worth doing. It takes courage to make such choices, and the exercise of that courage, in turn, further emboldens people.

A Mission that Matters of service to others further cements the team-binding power of striving to overcome tough challenges. True leadership is not just influencing, but influencing for the good. Likewise, teams not only need to be good, they need to be good for something. Teams and individuals respond to serving a cause greater than themselves. Regular reflection on the major "whys" of the team, willingness to sacrifice for the greater good, and providing regular support and encouragement to teammates all support and synergistically reinforce the courage to boldly Choose the Hard.

Purpose infused throughout the collective team psyche generates strong commitment for what the team does. Energy, excitement, passion, and emotional engagement with the venture are like sparks igniting the rocket engines to blast the team off the pad. Buy-in matters; it takes team involvement in finding and developing the purpose to generate the most dedication. Purpose imposed from outside is a less powerful energizer.

Deep engagement demands taking the work, but not yourself, very seriously. It requires the emotional risk of accepting vulnerability and is amplified when individuals step out of their comfort zones. High energy helps, although the team must guard against frenetic, wrong-direction activity. Meaningfulness and staying the course on activities that support the main purpose guard against ineffective, wheel-spinning excitement.

Although contagious, passion can also be quiet and deep. The key is to generate the most intense commitment, not the loudest cheering. Such deeply abiding dedication to the mission gives a team the aspirational vigor to energetically make things happen.

Overall, teams should carefully consider all the elements relating to purpose. These considerations form the first steps of however long a given team's journey may last. It's important to take those steps thoughtfully and with wise intent. Furthermore, along the arc of that journey, all team members need to keep hearkening back to those guides and use them to navigate when the pathways get rocky or seem to disappear in the underbrush.

People: The Who

People make or break any venture. Classic teambuilding activities acknowledge this reality. While it does focus on a crucial aspect, teambuilding by itself falls short. Building a team that conducts purposeful work is what matters. We people provide the creative, intellectual, and emotional engagement to start things off with purpose. We must maintain and expand the right outlooks and perspective to guide team development and actions. Who else to act, execute the program, and put the work into teamwork if not people, the dedicated individuals of a team?

Truly effective teamwork embraces the people connections to all the other elements. People connect and bind throughout all the four Ps. Everyone on the team, from the most senior leader to rookie, should constantly strive for awareness and appreciation of people principles while we organize, plan, prepare, and execute. That relationship orientation should always guide us.

Conceptualizing our team and those other teams with which we interact as "matrices to the nth power" keeps forefront in our mind the constant need to nourish and reinforce relationships. Every individual within each matrix is of incredible worth and deserves the utmost in respect, recognition, strengthening, and training development. Links come alive through positive, direct communications and conducting common and purposeful actions together. Links and nodes together, if strong, produce cohesion and unity.

Unquestionably, the most powerful unity-generating team factor is absolute trust. The higher the challenges before the team, the greater the need for that level of trust. To achieve this first-order trust requirement, all team members must consciously choose the zeroth-order precursor of being trustworthy. Team members willfully violating trust don't even deserve to remain on the team, though honest mistakes certainly are forgivable to a point.

Trustworthiness encompasses not just the utmost in integrity, but the best efforts to develop the highest skills and competence too. Capable humility, mutual support, and backup mentalities all contribute to expanding the trust beyond the baseline of unwavering integrity. Teams that meet these highest of trust standards are truly the dream crews with whom the best individuals would wish to serve.

The bottom line: people *are* the team! People cover for all the shortfalls everywhere else. Nothing gets conceived, nothing gets planned, and nothing gets done without the gems of the people on the team making it so. Teams exist for a purpose to implement a program with, hopefully, a wise perspective. Without caring for the people of the matrix to the nth power, program just does not get accomplished nearly as well.

Perspective: The How

Balanced, big-picture perspective should surround every concept, plan, and activity of the team. The abilities required to alternate between seeing the forest and each individual tree enable adjustments and improved productivity through adaptability. Overall effectiveness requires balance. Balance derives from perspective. Getting the nose up off the grindstone to assess the balance in viewpoint, effort, and attitude will enhance team performance.

Many characteristics contribute to balanced perspective. The right tone—positive and light in touch, though diligent in effort—appropriate humor, and conscious breaks in routine all serve to relieve stress and reenergize activity. A team culture where individuals don't take setbacks or critiques personally will enable the balanced perspective. With right attitudes, teams will reinforce natural human resiliency. Fitness and wellness positively promoted and valued offer additional balance benefits.

Exercising reality-grounded, golden-linings optimism empowers leaders to take on the tough challenges. This brand of optimism accepts, even relishes, dealing with real-world difficulties. Importantly, golden-linings optimism takes the view that the team operating diligently on correct principles will eventually overcome obstacles to success.

All real leaders must tether themselves to correct principles. Value-derived and incorporating foundational truths, correct principles set a gold standard for behavior and team activities. Principles-oriented perspective will protect against inherent organizational drift away from the route to mission accomplishment. Limiting the effects of errors in strategy, planning, and execution is crucial to success. Such a perspective requires constant assessment and prioritization. Is the team focused on the right thing, right now, as guided by the key principles?

Teams need to establish clear rules of behavior and performance within the group. Eager acceptance of high standards sets the best teams apart from the rest. Valuing the on-scene individual through reliance and trusting delegation amplifies team impact. Recognizing that who once was a rival could potentially become a partner creates a possibilities-perceiving viewpoint. Finally, staying tethered to one's individual and team values permits the ready admission of mistakes with the desire to use them as learning opportunities.

In the end, perspective comprises so many aspects that it's difficult to list them all, let alone fold every one into the team structure and activities. Nevertheless, we should incorporate as many aspects as we can. We need to perceive our team venture as a whole and see how it all fits together. Striving for balance feeds the perceptive team. Furthermore, the balanced team optimizes organization and performance across the entire spectrum of work and all the other 4P elements.

Program: The What, Where, and When

Program, process, procedures, or any number of other words describe the movement, action, and execution the team must complete to achieve success. Program means getting the work in teamwork done. All other 4P elements lead to program, producing activity that leads to pertinent results. The "fatherhood" of program resides in PAPA: Preparation, Awareness, Persistence, and Accountability. We can visualize these four qualities as satellites orbiting a central planet. The team that develops these characteristics will accelerate productive action.

Objective-Centric Operations form the Earth at the center of the PAPA orbit. You should craft objectives as carefully as any product or work that you undertake. Many guidelines exist to create useful objectives. One easily remembered framework is our first STARS pattern: Specific, Timelined, Actionable and Accounted for, Realistic, and Sensed. Objectives incorporating each of these elements will effectively guide positive execution.

Prioritization within and between objectives falls to the designated leader, with individual team members supporting and informing along the way. Some objectives are indeed more important than others. As well, some crucial objectives may not necessarily be direct objectives, but still serve an important supporting role.

Pace matters. Diligent, positive progress daily, while keeping the long-range view in mind too, enables the team to stay ahead of circumstances and the competition. Excellent pacing is tied to execution focus and does not happen by accident. The natural inclination is to tolerate delays and gradually fade from the necessary pace. Teams must consciously drive past that settling tendency with highly anticipatory outlooks. While operating today, well-paced teams concurrently evaluate lessons from the past to give corrections for the future.

In reality there are no true quick fixes. Quick pace and sense of urgency do not abrogate the requirement to do the job right. Teams should take the view that a problem is not truly fixed until it stays fixed.

It's OK to start with messy and disorganized ideas. Brainstorming, developing, and massaging those creative kernels will, as a process, contribute to getting and staying ahead. Coupled with an orientation where everyone on the team sees most challenges and issues as undeveloped opportunities, an abundance mentality will take hold. That mentality is not unrealistic, but instead allows capitalizing on the true opportunities in the workplace and marketplace.

"So what?" What's the relevance? Why and how does a given issue matter with respect to meeting the objectives and accomplishing the mission? Constant evaluation and introspection keep the team on track. It's no use being the leader of the pack in an intense cross-country race if you wander off onto the wrong trail while others behind stay on the right path. Staying on the correct path and pacing the team optimally, not necessarily to the all-out maximum, will produce the best overall execution performance over the long run.

Relentless preparation lays the foundation for all actions that will produce successful execution. When you begin to think you're ready, redouble your efforts, because invariably there's more to prepare. Plan, then replan. The second STARS pattern will guide the team's planning: Scenario, Tasks, Assess, Resources, and Steps. Leave no stone unturned.

Team members need to train diligently and continually, ideally via skills-based training. Mental ideation and rehearsals will leverage this aspect of preparation. Springing beyond training, formal and informal communications form the bridge between planning and action. The briefing, also using this same STARS pattern, sets the right tone and aligns the plan with execution. All communications, whether in formal briefing settings or not, should follow the C4 pattern: Clear, Complete, Concise, and Concrete.

The process to reach and maintain peak performance is far from easy. It takes effort, imagination, and a willingness to remain constantly on guard. Diligent preparation produces confident competence to counter the mediocrity of complacency. In turn, actively fighting complacency inspires the team to keep on a learning and improving path continually, forming a mutually reinforcing exchange between preparation and competence.

Growing from a trust culture, the best teams constantly question, learn, grow, and flourish in knowledge and skills. The Learning-Plus team enjoys competitive advantages of greater adaptability and confidence. Integral to such a culture is the almost compulsive desire to improve operations, team structure, and relationships. Mental simulations, rehearsals, and envisioning connect with more formal learning processes to drive performance to higher levels. Coupled with humbly admitting errors and then proactively engaging in mistake-driven learning, Learning-Plus teams arrive at much better results.

Performing the right preparation, the team will grow in awareness and understanding of every factor, positive and negative, that will affect operations. Situational awareness (SA) is a fruit of that preparation. SA allows the team to quickly note changes to the business baseline, then respond as appropriate. While a characteristic of high-performing individuals and teams, SA is also a skill that the team can continue to develop. Many factors enhance situational awareness, none more than direct, elegant approaches to problem solving.

With preparation and awareness providing capability, the team that exercises persistence will add the will to overcome. Capability plus willpower strengthens the team to execute all the way to successful completion. While persistence requires stubborn determination, really potent persistence acknowledges that some obstacles on a given pathway may prove insurmountable. The adaptive team then adjusts to find alternate routes to reaching objectives and fulfilling the mission.

Our teams must practice persistent adaptation. We should strive for alignment between our plans and actions at every juncture, recognizing that we will need to adapt constantly. The four-part format represented by the acronym MARS (Mindset, Act Aligned, Risk Mitigate, and Steps) will help us organize those heat-of-action adjustments.

Continually realigning requires rapid and precise adjustments, just like steering a rocket. Extensive internally and externally aligned communications play a crucial role in that process. Mitigating risks during execution requires that we expect the unexpected and cultivate "downside sensitivity." Even while staying optimistic, we should employ this tactic, which is an important component of high situational awareness.

Constantly comparing the steps taken during operations with the intended plan, or "guidance" in our spaceship metaphor, helps us replan and improve execution. It takes a patient, persistent attitude to improve continually as we focus on these "gimbaling" realignments.

A strong mindset of willingness to address problems quickly, with leaders setting the tone and all team members ideally supporting, contributes to an accountability culture. A team has its own velocity vector, consisting of the magnitude of pace pointed in a given direction. Ideally, all team members pull together and the overall team vector is pointed in an objective-attaining orientation. When it drifts, we must honestly accept responsibility and then realign it.

Externally mandated accountability exists on multiple legal, regulatory, and policy levels. Internally, teams should exercise honest shared accountability as well. Within such a team-directed internal accountability culture, team members willingly accept individual responsibilities. Everyone recognizes that such willingness is a powerful team effort enhancer.

To further refine accountability culture, teams should focus on unified, results-oriented communications. A powerful subset of accountability, focused communications require regular, structured debriefings of operations and activities. Investing the time and effort to do so will, invariably, improve future execution. In fact, pertinent learning from a debriefing can prove as beneficial to the team as completing a given operation or event itself. The down-to-EARTH debriefing framework includes Execution, Accountability, Review, Timeline, and Highlights.

The Teamwork and Leadership Connection: Influence and Impact

Teamwork and leadership intersect and mutually support one another. They really are two sides of the same coin, the currency to accomplish worthwhile Mission that Matters endeavors. Enlightened leaders encourage and empower teams. In turn, effective teams serve to nurture and develop powerful leaders. It's no accident that true "influencers for good" arise most often from team settings.

Sometimes we place our leaders on pedestals, assuming that leadership is a rare, innate gift exercised from some stratospheric perch. We all know of incredible leaders with such gifts. Hopefully you've had the privilege, as I've had, to work directly with such outstanding individuals. However, in deliberately and diligently learning and applying correct principles, we all can grow our influence—regardless of innate ability. Leadership is, after all, the power to influence others to get things done. Accordingly, it includes many skills that one can learn and refine. Also, leadership that matters inspires in team members a desire to serve others with a purpose beyond self.

With growth in power to influence comes increasingly more impact. Few individuals, in and of themselves, gather sufficient influence to have significant impact on the world. The days of the lone eagle business hero are mostly gone. The interconnected, worldwide, 24/7 business environment also necessitates flatter, less hierarchal structures. These modern company frameworks require more, not less, leadership, broadly distributed throughout the entire organization. Accordingly, the enlightened trend toward operating in self-directed teams continues to grow. Invariably, you will need to contribute meaningfully to the success of multiple team ventures to also succeed as an individual.

It's been a great source of personal joy and professional gratification for me to have been a part of numerous incredible teams in many different ventures. I've relished being a leader in those operational settings and look back with deep gratitude for the opportunities that have been granted me to lead. With colleagues and dear friends in teams, we've made a difference with powerful impacts, both tangible and intangible. While most of those ventures have been in a unique and specialized field, where few experience the environment firsthand, the principles for success and team progress are exactly the same as in any team venture.

Hopefully, in distilling for this work execution leadership and teamwork lessons from all those years in the field, the influence and positive impact will continue. I'm an action-oriented "do leader." However, the process of writing this book has reinforced to me the value of "thought leadership," influencing others for good via the written and spoken word. I've attempted to exercise the right amount and kind of thought leadership here. It's been an invigorating intellectual exercise. Ideally, it will resonate with you and give practical, usable benefits.

Your best opportunities to grow professionally, then to influence more expansively, and ultimately to produce impactful results, will come in team settings. Seek them out; engage enthusiastically whether as the newest rookie or seasoned veteran. Exercise leadership whether officially appointed as leader or not. Consider that a key leadership competency is also to be a supportive team player. Ponder the key principles you must apply. Then, without reservation, practice them consistently. The effort and practice will make all the difference, professionally and personally.

A last quote, one that is cited quite often, is necessary. I include this particular quote because it captures, more than any other I've ever seen, the essence of dedicated operational effort. While President Teddy Roosevelt expressed these thoughts in the first person male singular, it applies perfectly well to the collective in the magnificently diverse world of today's business teams. Consider it a tribute to you, your teammates, and all you do in the quest for execution success:

> The credit belongs to the man who is actually in the arena, whose face is marred by dust and sweat and blood; who strives valiantly; who errs, who comes short again and again, because there is no effort without error and shortcoming; but who does actually strive to do the deeds; who knows great enthusiasms, the great devotions; who spends himself in a worthy cause; who at the best knows in the end the triumph of high achievement, and who at the worst, if he fails, at least fails while daring greatly, so that his place shall never be with those cold and timid souls who neither know victory nor defeat.

It's my sincere desire that the principles in this book will strongly influence you and positively impact your teams. In hopeful anticipation, I confidently believe diligent application of universal principles of leadership for execution excellence will make a difference. I may not be able to join you directly on your own missions, but I like to believe I will have contributed to your success.

So, like Dr. Goddard, take your dreams from hopes to reality. I wish you the very best for magnificent team triumphs in the purposeful pursuit of effective business execution.

A FUNNY THING HAPPENED ON THE WAY TO THE LAUNCH PAD

Biography

Astronaut Rick Searfoss shares with only a handful of people the sublime joys of flying in space. In his career, he has continually served in dynamic, high-impact operational organizations. Rick has led many teams, including commanding the STS-90 Neurolab life science research mission on space shuttle *Columbia*. He piloted *Atlantis* on mission STS-76, a joint Russian-American mission to the *Mir* space station. His first space flight was as pilot of *Columbia* on STS-58, a Spacelab mission and the first two-week duration space shuttle flight. In the Astronaut Corps and the Air Force, Colonel Searfoss held numerous leadership positions with execution responsibilities for producing team results.

For over a decade, Rick has run his own business as a high-content expert speaker and consultant on the topics of leadership, teamwork, execution, innovation, and peak performance. His extensive leadership experience and work with some of today's most innovative companies let him fulfill his mission of sharing teamwork, leadership, and innovation lessons of human spaceflight with business leaders worldwide. The websites www.ricksearfoss.com and www. astronautspeaker.com highlight his professional speaker offerings.

Prior to becoming an astronaut, Colonel Searfoss was a fighter pilot and test pilot in the US Air Force with over 6,100 hours flying time in eighty-four different types of aircraft. He is also a Distinguished Graduate of the Air Force Fighter Weapons School and the US Naval Test Pilot School. Concurrent with his business activities, Rick is also Director of Flight Test Operations and Chief Test Pilot for XCOR Aerospace, helping to develop the Lynx suborbital spaceplane. In this role, he has test flown multiple technology demonstrator prototypes and piloted more flights in rocket-powered craft than anyone else on the planet. He also instructs advanced jet handling in Impala Jet and Sabreliner aircraft for Flight Research, Inc.

Colonel Searfoss graduated first in his class from the United States Air Force Academy in 1978, earning the Harmon, Fairchild, Price, and Tober awards as number one overall, in academics, engineering, and the aeronautical engineering major. He later earned a master of science degree in aeronautics from the California Institute of Technology on a National Science Foundation Fellowship and graduated from Air Force Squadron Officer School, Air Command and Staff College, and Air War College.

Rick's numerous other awards include the Air Force Distinguished Flying Cross, the Legion of Merit, Defense Meritorious and Superior Service Medals, Air Force Meritorious Service and Commendation Medals, NASA Exceptional Service and Outstanding Leadership Medals, USAF Squadron Officer School Commandant's Trophy as number one graduate in his class, Air Force Aero Propulsion Laboratory Excellence in Turbine Engine Design Award, Tactical Air Command F-111 Instructor Pilot of the Year, Outstanding Young Men of America, and Eagle Scout.

Rick and his wife Julie have three daughters and three young grandsons. Although he loves his professional activities, nothing compares to playing with the grandsons! He also enjoys running, backpacking, and model aircraft. With little musical ability himself but having married into a very talented family, Rick loves being in the audience whenever his immediate and extended family members share their incredible musical and dance talents.

Personal Insight: The Individual Path

I am a child of both the Jet Age and Apollo Era. My early childhood coincided with the heyday of military jet aviation, with exotic new designs regularly lighting up the skies. Nothing could stop the US Air Force from going higher, faster, and farther than ever before. Growing up in that environment as the son of an Air Force officer, the sheer energy and boundless confidence grabbed hold of me and never let go. From the earliest I can remember, I yearned to become a jet pilot like my dad.

It seems like an inordinate number of our family pictures when I was young show me holding a model airplane. On occasions when Dad brought home his flight gear, he'd need to put it out of reach so little Ricky wouldn't grab his helmet and plop it on his much too small head. Hooking up the mask, catching its rubbery odor faintly mixed with jet fuel and sweat, then lowering the dark visor to see the world like a pilot, my imagination would soar into the wild blue yonder. Nothing, absolutely nothing, could ever be cooler than flying jets.

Or could it? Exactly one month before my fifth birthday, America's human spaceflight adventure began. On May 5, 1961, Alan Shepard climbed into a tiny little capsule, *Freedom 7*, perched atop a Redstone rocket. The launch team "lit the candle." Shepard screamed off the launch pad, heading east over the Atlantic on the way to 116 miles high. He accelerated to more than 5,000 miles per hour, flying 300 miles in just fifteen minutes. Even to this four-year old, it was obvious America had a team that could accomplish amazing things: NASA.

We could've readily beat the Russians, who had launched Yuri Gagarin less than a month prior on April 12. However, Wernher von Braun's disciplined team had added one extra unmanned test flight, just to be sure. The Soviet Union seized the window of opportunity to launch Yuri. The Soviets got to take credit for the first man in space. Then, because of the ensuing public alarm that they had won that stage of the space race, we kicked our nation's program into the highest gear possible. Had we gone first, it's possible we would not have felt as compelled to shoot for the moon so aggressively. Purpose-driven execution success requires that imperative sense of urgency.

Regardless, the combination of amazing hardware, rockets that men actually flew, and the omnipresent and growing public attention, made a huge impression on this kindergartner. By the time the Gemini Program was launching, I had connected the dots that the astronauts were really military pilots, like my dad. That closed the deal. I was going to be a jet pilot *and* an astronaut. By age eight, the dream was born. Mind you, I had no clue of how to get there, but the power of that inspiration led the way for decisions about what I would do and how hard I would work along the way.

I followed every detail of the space program, mostly intrigued by the hardware and engineering of it all. The astronaut dream, though it mostly seemed a distant and not quite possible prospect, informed decisions and prompted diligence all the way through my youth. I continued to build model airplanes and rockets, discovering in fifth grade something called physics that explained how they all worked, in glorious and exciting detail. Amazing, it's not just magic! Dig down and study hard. You have to do well in math also to really get this stuff. One step at a time. "I'm going to the Air Force Academy," I announced to my mother one day when I was in seventh grade. "Lots of astronauts went to West Point and the Naval Academy, but I think in the future more astronauts will be from the Air Force Academy." My mom replied, "Fine, son, but mow the lawn first."

America by then had successfully completed Gemini, built the humongous *Saturn V* rocket, and geared up to win the moon race. At age thirteen, on July 20, 1969, I watched on a tiny black-and-white television, together with a couple hundred other Boy Scouts at New Hampshire's Camp Carpenter, as Neil Armstrong stepped out onto the surface of the moon. Along with the whole world, we held our breath as we witnessed the culminating technical achievement of human history. NASA had demonstrated the pinnacle of effective execution. Leadership, teamwork, and plain-old hard work had fulfilled President Kennedy's vision and purpose.

My individual preparation from there mirrored that of many other astronauts: top grades, engineering academic major, fulfilling my seventh grade goal of graduating from the Air Force Academy. Somehow, when I pulled the nose up off the grindstone after four years as a cadet, I led my class of 981 people as the top graduate overall, in academics, engineering, and in the aeronautical engineering major. I figured none of that would hurt when I applied to be an astronaut. Coincidentally, 1978, the year of my graduation, marked the first space shuttle astronaut class also. Lo and behold, it included Air Force Academy graduates, even an aero major or two. I determined that perhaps this dream was maybe not an impossibility after all, a few years down track.

Graduate school at the California Institute of Technology, Air Force pilot training, operational attack pilot flying, sitting alert in England, instructing in Idaho, US Navy Test Pilot School as a USAF exchange officer, finally to Air Force flight test at Edwards Air Force Base, California. I'd finally made it to the home of all those higher, faster, farther records that had so jazzed me as a youth! After many years of hard work, I was living my earliest dream to be an Air Force test pilot. Daily on the flight line, I experienced that kerosene-like jet fuel odor, climbed into the cockpits of many types of aircraft, sweated in ecstatic exertion as I took them through their paces, breathed through a rubber mask, and saw the world from the wild blue yonder as the test pilot I'd finally become. This dream come true was the result of studying and preparing for untold hours, following a plan that I had discerned at an early age, and competing with other hard-driving overachievers.

Eventually, I received a life-changing phone call in January 1990 when Don Puddy, Johnson Space Center Flight Crew Operations Director, came on the line and asked, in his smooth, bass voice and Texas accent, "Rick, how'd you like to come on down to JSC and work for me in the Astronaut Office?" My immediate response: "I'll be there tomorrow if you want!" Interesting implication in the way Don's question was worded. He didn't ask me if I wanted to fly in space, but instead whether I wanted to work as part of his team. As I was soon to learn, the program was really about hard work and pooling the efforts of very talented people to execute well in a complex and challenging operational environment. The flying in space part of it for an individual astronaut was really just the icing on the cake of getting the mission done. NASA's human spaceflight operations represented team execution excellence, with the best of the best.

Evolution toward Purpose: The Team Path

All the while with the individual efforts, I was also following a parallel and equally important preparation path with every team effort of which I was a part. Unknown to me, that path also prepared me for astronaut duty—more than I would appreciate until I was in the program. The selection board of eight astronauts and four senior NASA officials really drilled down to discern if a given candidate would fit in and work well in team settings, regardless of individual accomplishments. As I look back on the hour-long interview with the board and how much I enjoyed it, I recognize that my sincere appreciation for teams that executed well certainly showed in our discussion. Furthermore, my years of previous team experiences, as much as all the technical background, served magnificently in astronaut crewmember performance once selected.

The first team interaction I ever remember came roughly the same time as that indelible experience of seeing Alan Shepard launch into space. Our parents had just dropped my sister and me off at the base childcare center. I was nervous, well out of my comfort zone, and did not want to be left in that forbidding environment. I remember my little sister, Debbie, two years my junior, encouraging me, "Don't worry, Ricky, we'll be OK together." And we were. Over the next few hours, I warmed up to the setting and did fine. I've always remembered her early empathetic, sisterly kindness, and to me it captures the essence of the best teams: "We'll be OK together."

Growing up as a typical middle-class kid (except that as an Air Force brat I moved more than most), I engaged in many youth activities: Little League baseball, Boy Scouts, clubs, school drama, band, church youth groups, high school soccer and track, and the like. I discovered early on that I really enjoyed getting things done with others. I was never one for just hanging out, but when connected with other likeminded people with a mission in mind, even a simple, juvenile one, I came alive. Scouts in particular appealed to me, and with the guidance of some superb adult leaders, my parents, and team support within a terrific troop, I completed my Eagle Scout award. In retrospect, the leadership and team opportunities in those settings were prolific. I can honestly say that the most important principles I used commanding a human spaceflight I had learned as a twelve-year-old Boy Scout patrol leader.

Along with providing a sterling academic education, the United States Air Force Academy is one of our nation's foremost leadership development institutions. Virtually every single aspect of the experience ties to team execution. Even individual academic expertise connects to teams, as squadrons are ranked by collective academic standing. I was fortunate my first, toughest year to belong to the top squadron out of forty in these rankings. As a team, we worked hard to maintain that spot, and those who understood a particular subject more readily than others freely tutored squadron mates. After my first semester, it helped ease my intense first-year experience with the upperclassmen in "Blackjack 21" squadron to contribute a 4.0 grade point average to that cause.

I loved the multiple team settings in all we did at the Academy: academics, military training and drill, sports, airmanship, and more. Although the program was difficult, succeeding with classmates, who along the way became the best of friends, really made it all worthwhile. My squadron mates and classmates from my upper-class squadron, "Viking 9," remain, along with my spaceflight crewmates, my nearest and dearest friends. As tough as a service academy education is, it also, for me, bolstered the "heart" side of leadership. I saw firsthand over and over the kind of "leaders eat last" examples that I was determined to emulate.

A key Air Force Academy axiom is "cooperate and graduate." Within the boundaries of a very strict honor code where cadets must individually complete much of their work, like tests and papers, the philosophy builds leaders who deeply understand how teams get results. I remember finishing a several-day long survival training exercise where we had to evade and escape through the mountains while being chased as if we had ejected behind enemy lines. None of us had eaten more than a few ounces of survival rations for days, but somehow one or two bites of my cornflake bar still remained. As we reconvened at the end of the exercise, I came across my friend and classmate Jim Weidmann, one of the biggest, toughest guys in our class and a football standout. With over 250 pounds of mass to try to nourish, Jim's rations had been gone for days, and he looked about ready to pass out. It never occurred to me not to offer up immediately my paltry few bites, and he gobbled the remnants of the ration bar right down. It was not that big a deal really, just one of many thousands upon thousands of contributing leadership, teambuilding, and mutual support interactions each class accumulates on the four-year journey to commissioning as Air Force officers.

Air Force Academy stories could continue for several pages, with many great learning points. I mentioned a few here only because they formed a core foundation for my later leadership practice. The anecdotes and examples throughout this book came primarily from my more unique space experiences. One crucial caveat applies to every single example in this book though, regardless of origin. While the experiences themselves may be rare, the leadership and execution principles employed within those unique team settings are universal, applicable to any undertaking.

A Life-Changing Awareness Expansion

I graduated from the US Naval Test Pilot School at the end of 1988. The year-long program proved the most intense flying and academic experience of my career—effectively a PhD in flying. Test Pilot School is unquestionably the most difficult military flying training program in existence. Particularly as an Air Force pilot, it wasn't just about learning how to become a test pilot, but also adapting to the differing Navy culture and way of operating. My final project report, due a mere two weeks after completing four test flights of the Swedish Draken fighter, was over one hundred pages long. It didn't reduce the stress or difficulty any when my wife had to undergo a major neurosurgical procedure at Bethesda Naval Hospital while we were in the program. Everyone was very relieved on graduation night! My commanders had allowed me to represent the Air Force with our sister service, and I had done well. I had now filled all the major squares to enable me finally to apply to the astronaut program. It was a huge milestone in my life.

Although a key professional landmark, completing Test Pilot School was a different type of life-changing experience from one that was to happen a short time later. In 1989, when it first came out, a family member gave me the gift of Dr. Stephen R. Covey's *The 7 Habits of Highly Effective People*. What an epiphany! I had never read any other self-development book before. What jumped out about this book was how perfectly descriptive it was. By then, I had enjoyed many great leadership and operational execution experiences. I had a deep reservoir of examples from all the teams of which I'd been a part growing up, during the Air Force Academy leadership development cauldron, and in my flying career. I reflected on every superb leader under whom I had served, the multiple successful teams of which I'd been a part, and the times when I had proven my own leadership and teambuilding capabilities. Invariably those remembrances all pointed to the same key operative principles that Covey highlighted.

Given that I saw firsthand in previous team environments how descriptive these factors were, I was determined to intentionally apply them in my future endeavors. By this point, I'd been promoted to the rank of major in the Air Force and begun to assume greater leadership roles. The active cultivation of those habits paid off. Then, when selected for the Astronaut Corps, I figured that my teams and spaceflight crews would also benefit if I continued to incorporate these vital habits. Gaining that experience further opened up my eyes to the power of the human, less tangible and technical side, while prompting me to read other similar books. I still continue that practice, trying to absorb at least one or two business books a month, but none has ever resonated with me quite so powerfully.

Along the way, once assigned to crews, somehow I won the lottery with two of the absolute best mission commanders ever in the American human space program. Colonel John Blaha and General Kevin Chilton, both of whom you read about in the book, are also Air Force Academy graduates. They were phenomenally talented technically as astronauts and pilots. Furthermore, unlike some commanders, they coupled their talents with the most caring and team-inspiring leadership possible. John's and Chili's mentoring accelerated my own continuing leadership development and team orientation far beyond what I could've imagined when I first showed up for astronaut training.

Finally, I had the chance to use everything about teams and leadership I had ever learned in commanding the STS-90 Neurolab mission, a five-hundred-million-dollar flight on the two-billion-dollar space shuttle *Columbia* with seven lives on the line. I rolled an entire life of execution leadership development and service in pursuit of a greater purpose into that command, the most gratifying and overall challenging experience of my career. It was the most incredible privilege I could imagine to be granted command of an American space mission, to mold a seven-person crew, including five rookies, into a cohesive team, and along with them influence for good many hundreds of people who supported the undertaking. The STS-90 mission was the most complex human space research mission ever flown, the only space shuttle flight out of all 135 to produce a book of peer-reviewed, leading-edge science results. It was as successful within its focused realm as any space mission ever. I'm grateful to have been a key team builder and leader within the Neurolab universe.

Just a few months after STS-90, as mentioned earlier, I met Dr. Covey, who provided counsel that closed the loop on the original life-changing experience of reading his seminal work nine years before. I had direct advice from the man himself, and it instantly transported my confidence to a deeper level of understanding and potential application. I really did have something significant to offer. I had been incredibly blessed with many powerful leadership and team lessons. With the right preparation and continuing hard work, I could also share them effectively in new settings.

Adventures and Ventures

In my post-astronaut career, I've enjoyed a wide variety of different ventures. Some are, like my spaceflights, also great adventures. With each, I seek to engage with likeminded individuals in intensive team undertakings having demanding requirements for execution success. Somehow, I've been able to throw together an eclectic mix of activities. Technical consulting, active test flying, and "New Space" private aerospace ventures have all figured prominently in my post-astronaut work. I've even had the chance to do some movie consulting and a little on-camera work, introducing a documentary, appearing in a Volkswagen commercial, and having a cameo appearance in one of the Hollywood movies for which I consulted.

Most relevant to Dr. Covey's counsel, though, for over a decade now I've focused on sharing leadership, teamwork, peak performance, and innovation lessons with the business world as a professional speaker. In full realization that human spaceflight is not just an adventure but an operational venture with incredibly relevant leadership and teamwork lessons, I've sought influence and impact. My personal communications mission is to share business-relevant lessons of human spaceflight with whomever will benefit. As one of barely five hundred humans ever to have enjoyed the experience of space flight, with the added skill of being an effective storyteller, I see it as a joyful duty. I've always loved to tell stories, whether with other pilots, to my daughters as they grew up, now to young grandsons, or on stage in front of thousands of people. I love the personal engagement. I even see it as a form of leadership and teambuilding to open oneself up and share deeply with an audience. It has been an amazing journey to interact with and serve clients and audiences from virtually every industry.

The funny thing that happened to this hyper-focused individual on the way to the launch pad is that I discovered the power of teams. Even in parallel with a life of concentrated technical pursuits and individual accomplishments, I enjoyed from early on the feelings and synergies that exist in high-performing teams. While trained as an engineer, I've always also been, in a sense, a "recovering engineer," thinking about and dedicated to the intangible human side of any venture. These days, those human-relations thoughts predominate. Even in the technical teams to which I contribute with expertise or test-flying skills, what now gratifies me most is seeing my teams grow and develop as we break new ground and achieve our collective dreams.

Glossary

Execution Excellence

4P Peak Performance Balance: Purpose, People, Perspective, Program.

C4 Communications: Clear, Complete, Concise, Concrete.

EARTH Productive Debriefings: Execution, Accountability, Review, Timeline (and Timely), Highlights.

MARS Route to Active Aligned Execution: Mindset, Act Aligned, Risk Mitigate, Steps.

PAPA Execution Orbit: Preparation, Awareness, Persistence, Accountability.

SA: Situational Awareness

STARS (1) Objectives Definition: Specific, Timelined, Actionable and Accounted For, Realistic, Sensed.

STARS (2) Planning Framework: Scenario, Tasks, Assess, Resources, Steps.

NASA, Space Shuttle, and Military Aviation

ATO: Abort to Orbit. A main engine failure emergency procedure that required firing the OMS engines to assist in reaching orbit.

CAPCOM: Capsule Communicator. The astronaut on console in the MCC who speaks directly to the crew in space.

CDR: Commander. An experienced pilot astronaut, occupying the front left seat of the shuttle for launch and reentry, performing technical duties with DPS, life support, GNC, and landing the orbiter, as well as having overall responsibility for mission safety and success.

DPS: Data Processing System. Integrated system of all the space shuttle computer hardware and software. The orbiter's nervous system.

EI: Entry Interface. The point in a space shuttle reentry where the returning orbiter is considered to first encounter the atmosphere, at roughly 400,000 feet altitude.

EVA: Extravehicular Activity. A spacewalk.

FDF: Flight Data File. All the onboard checklists, manuals, and documentation for astronaut crews to do their jobs.

GNC: Guidance, Navigation, and Control. The essential hardware, software, and sensors to know where the spaceship is, where you want it to go, and how you'll get there.

GPC: General Purpose Computer. One of five main computers per orbiter to control and monitor space shuttle trajectories, systems, and payloads.

HUD: Heads-Up Display. An optical device used in some advanced military and civilian aircraft, as well as the space shuttle, that projects critical flight information right in front of the pilot's forward external view to quickly allow interpretation of data while still looking outside.

IFM: In-Flight Maintenance. Specific crew activities to repair space shuttle systems in orbit.

ISS: International Space Station.

JSC: Johnson Space Center in Houston, Texas. Where the astronauts live, work, and train.

KSC: Kennedy Space Center, on the east coast of Florida. NASA's primary launch site. Known colloquially as "The Cape."

LCC: Launch Control Complex. The facility at KSC for monitoring and controlling every aspect of a space shuttle until it clears the pad after launch, at which point control is transferred to MCC in Houston.

MECO: Main Engine Cutoff. Engine shutdown at the end of the ascent to orbit.

MCC: Mission Control Center. The facility at JSC from where human space missions are controlled. For every controller in the "front room," there would be an entire unseen technical support "back room" team elsewhere. Alternately called "Mission Control" or, when calling from space, "Houston," the MCC controlled missions from tower clear at launch until reaching a certain point in the post-landing checklist, at which time control reverted back to the LCC at KSC.

MEEP: *Mir* Environmental Effects Payload. A specialized engineering experiment placed on the outside of the Russian *Mir* space station during a spacewalk on mission STS-76.

MS 2: Mission Specialist Two. Flight engineer crew member for launch and reentry, seated on the orbiter flight deck between and aft of the front two seats.

NASA: National Aeronautics and Space Administration.

OMS: Orbital Maneuvering System. The two 6,000-pound-thrust rocket engines, plus associated plumbing and propellant tanks, used to maneuver in space and deorbit for reentry.

PLT: Pilot. Second in command on a space shuttle mission, occupying the front right seat for launch and reentry, performing technical duties with main engines, OMS, RCS, hydraulic and electrical systems, fuel cells, and more. Backup crewmember for landing the shuttle.

RCRS: Regenerative Carbon Dioxide Removal System. A life support system developed in the 1990s and flown on some long-duration missions late in the Space Shuttle Program. The RCRS saved substantial weight and stowage volume in allowing a drastic reduction in the number of lithium hydroxide canisters previously used to absorb cabin atmosphere carbon dioxide.

RCS: Reaction Control System. Thirty-eight primary 870-pound-thrust and six vernier 24-pound-thrust rocket engines, plumbing, and fuel and oxidizer tanks for orbiter attitude control, station keeping, and close-in maneuvering.

RMS: Remote Manipulator System. The space shuttle's robotic arm.

RSS: Rotating Service Structure. The portion of the space shuttle launch pad that wrapped around the shuttle to protect it and allow access for servicing prelaunch. The RSS was typically rolled back the day prior to launch.

SLF: Shuttle Landing Facility. A three-mile long runway carved out of Florida swampland at KSC for orbiters returning from space and conventional aircraft operations supporting the NASA mission.

SRB: Solid Rocket Booster. One of the two white, side-mounted boosters of a space shuttle system, each containing over a million pounds of solid propellant.

SST: Single-System Trainer. One of many small training facilities at JSC set up to provide training on one space shuttle system at a time. SST work was always a precursor to full-up simulator training.

STA: Shuttle Training Aircraft. A highly modified Grumman Gulfstream II business jet, set up to handle just like the space shuttle, for CDRs and PLTs to practice approaches and landings as realistically as possible.

TFS: Tactical Fighter Squadron. In military aviation, the squadron is the basic operational execution unit. In the US Air Force, fighter and attack jet squadrons were given the TFS designation between 1958 and 1991. In 1991 it was shortened to FS, for Fighter Squadron. TFS is used in this book as it reflects the timeframe during which I served in such squadrons.

VAB: Vehicle Assembly Building. The iconic, 526 foot tall, cube-shaped building at KSC where Saturn V and full-up space shuttle "stacks" were assembled. At one time the largest building by volume in the world, the American flag painted on its side is larger than a football field.

WSO: Weapons System Officer. A non-pilot aircrew member, initially trained as a navigator but then also becoming expert in radar and other sensor use, weapons employment, and electronic warfare. WSOs serve in two-place tactical aircraft like the F-4 Phantom, F-111 Aardvark, or F-15E Strike Eagle.

REFERENCES

Cathcart, Jim. *The Acorn Principle.* New York: St. Martin's Press, 1998.

Covey, Stephen R. *The Seven Habits of Highly Effective People: Powerful Lessons in Personal Change.* New York: Free Press, 1989.

Curphy, Gordon J., Robert C. Ginnett, and Robert L. Hughes. *Leadership: Enhancing the Lessons of Experience.* Boston: McGraw Hill, 2006.

Klein, Gary. *Sources of Power: How People Make Decisions.* Cambridge, Massachusetts: The MIT Press, 1998.